As the Days of
Noah

Charles Edmond McCraw Jr

As the Days of
Noah

CHARLES EDMOND MCCRAW JR

ARPress

ILLUMINATING IDEAS
EMPOWERING VOICES

ARPress
45 Dan Road Suite 5
Canton MA 02021
Hotline: 1(888) 821-0229
Fax: 1(508) 545-7580

Ordering Information:
Quantity sales. Special discounts are available on quantity purchases by corporations, associations, and others. For details, contact the publisher at the address above.

Printed in the United States of America.

ISBN-13:   Softcover   979-8-89676-255-3

                   eBook   979-8-89676-256-0

Library of Congress Control Number: 2025904683

Contents

INTRODUCTION I

CHAPTER 1 GOD 1

CHAPTER 2 NOAH 27

CHAPTER 3 THE BUILDING OF THE ARK 49

CHAPTER 4 THE RISE OF THE ARK 73

CHAPTER 5 THE FLOATING OF THE ARK 97

CHAPTER 6 THE DOVE AND THE OLIVE LEAF 121

CHAPTER 7 THE DESCENT OF THE ARK 147

CHAPTER 8 BOW IN THE CLOUDS 171

INTRODUCTION

I will start by saying God bless you and that I hope these words in this book will be of hope, help, and that you will be even amazed at what you about to read.

As the days of Noah is like a restaurant that has an all-you-can-eat buffet: the food you want to eat, or will eat, because there is some food on the buffet you might not like. You will find meat, veggies, fruit, dessert, and much more.

This table for the family has been prepared with everyone's taste in mind. We eat, we fellowship, we enjoy one another, regardless of the differences in taste. There is another meal every person needs to eat: the Word of God.

Matthew 4:4 KJV tells us that.

The Word of God is one book to fill your heart, soul, and mind. Believers get different portions of the meal from the Word of God.

There are many different denominations believing or receiving portions of the meal from the Word of God, but regardless of whether it is milk or meat, there is one thing we all must agree on: how to be saved.

Romans 10:9–10 tells of how we become family of God and set at another table with our Lord and King.

I said all this to say this: One might not like all that in this book. Some might like it all.

God welcome all the rich, poor, tall, short, skinny, overweight, beautiful, ugly, worst sinner, the less sinner, the evilest hearted, and the gentle at his table as long as he come by the romans road of believing his son Jesus died for ones sins in his heart and confess with his mouth.

Enjoy the meal and eat what you can; chew what you can; put aside what you cannot—maybe you can eat it later.

You are going to see how Noah's days from God, Satan, the ark, building of the ark, the flood, raise of the ark, floating of the ark, dove and olive branch, and descending of the ark run parallel with our grace period, tribulation period, millennium period, resurrection period, the battle of Lord Jesus and Satan, New Jerusalem, how Satan is building his kingdom and army and more.

All this knowledge, understanding, and even the ability to draft this book was made possible by my Heavenly Father spirit given me the understand in rightly dividing the Word of God.

I want to thank my Heavenly Father, especially for trusting this task to me to accomplish.

God bless and enjoy.

CHAPTER 1

GOD

Malachi 3:6

"For I am the LORD, I change not; therefore ye sons of Jacob are not consumed."

Hebrews 13:8

Jesus Christ is the same yesterday, today, and forever.

This tells me God in the beginning, Noah's days, in my time and the future will act, respond, correct, reward, and judge no different, so I can study God through his Word to see who he is in character, leadership, as creator, and more.

It is important to see the parallels between Noah's days and our times and events, past, present, and future, because unlike God, we humankind change our behavior, character, likes, dislikes, and emotions, and we undergo many changes throughout time. I can say humankind was not the same yesterday as today and definitely will not be forever, but God is the same today as in the past and the future to be able to see and understand his reason and action for what he has already done, is doing, and will do in the future.

I know God's anger and judgment happened in Noah's days. God's anger will happen in the future too.

I am going to compare Noah's days to our time and show how every event in Noah's days is a lively portrait of the things to come in our times as well as in Jesus's days, the body of Christ, the Rapture, the seven-year tribulation, the millennium, the two last witnesses, details of Satan's kingdom and army, New Jerusalem, supper time in heaven, and more.

I like what Jonah said about God.

Jonah 4:2 "And he prayed unto the Lord, and said, I pray thee, O Lord, was not this my saying, when I was yet in my country? Therefore I fled before unto Tarshish: for I knew that thou art a gracious God, and merciful, slow to anger, and of great kindness, and repentant thee of the evil."

Jonah in his anger just described God, who had destroyed humankind by flooding the whole planet before Jonah's time.

This speaks volume to me about God. He is gracious, merciful, slow to anger, of great kindness, and repentant of evil.

Jonah 3:10 "And God saw their works, that they turned from their evil way; and God repented of the evil, that he had said that he would do unto them; and he did it not."

I see so much here, and God is truly great and awesome. He is dealing with his servant Jonah on issues he needs to overcome but at the same time is dealing with an ungodly nation. God is showing his wisdom here as a leader and a father.

Jonah and God are acting as son and father. This is how a father would act toward his son to teach him important lessons.

I like what God said to him.

Jonah 4:9–11 "⁹And God said to Jonah, Does thou well to be angry for the gourd? And he said, I do well to be angry, even unto death. ¹⁰Then said the Lord, Thou hast had pity on the gourd, for the which thou hast not labored, neither maddest it grow; which came up in a night, and perished in a night: ¹¹And should not I spare Nineveh, that great city, wherein are more than six score thousand persons that cannot discern between their right hand and their left hand; and also much cattle?"

I can see the gentleness in God toward Jonah as his son.

The whole event with God and Jonah is like a relationship. God behaves as a father would when his son throws a hissy fit. He would put him in time-out till he calms down. The whale was Jonah's time-out. Jonah also knew how God was in his character and way of reacting, which tells me that a long-time relation had been going on between the two.

God is the same always, but there was no changing his mind when dealing with humankind in Noah's days or when the tribulation comes. It is not because he is not slow to anger, kind, merciful, and gentle.

Jonah has shown me a lot about God.

God never changes, so the same way God worked with Jonah he will do toward his born-again children. God knew Jonah and wanted to work on and change a fault in him by using his wisdom, love, patience, and power to do it, and it worked because Jonah was not the same after that lesson from God because he drafted the Book of Jonah in a third person. This was because the person he was writing about was not the same man drafting the book. Like he said in Philippians 1:6, "Being confident of this very thing, that he which hath begun a good work in you will perform it until the day of Jesus Christ."

This gives me a better understanding of how God really is working on me. The way God was dealing with Jonah is a good example; knowing Jonah's anger, he did not destroy Jonah, but with his wisdom changed the way Jonah thought and behaved toward his enemy. This is what God is doing in my time as well as with future believers.

This makes me confident of the answer to a question that God asked in Genesis 18:14:

"Is anything too hard for the Lord? At the time appointed I will return unto thee, according to the time of life, and Sarah shall have a son."

Jeremiah 32:17, "Ah Lord God! behold, thou hast made the heaven and the earth by thy great power and stretched out arm, and there is nothing too hard for thee."

Jeremiah gives the answer: no.

Looking at Abram before his name was changed to Abraham, God started working on him, but after God called him. It is the same with my time during this grace period.

Genesis 12:17–20

> [17]And the Lord plagued Pharaoh and his house with great plagues because of Sarai Abram's wife. 18And Pharaoh called Abram and said, what is this that thou hast done unto me? why didst thou not tell me that she was thy wife? [19]Why saidst thou, she is my sister? so I might have taken her to me to wife: now therefore behold thy wife, take her, and go thy way. [20]And Pharaoh commanded his men concerning him: and they sent him away, and his wife, and all that he had.

I notice God did not deal with Abram but with pharaoh, who immediately restored Sarai, but why, I wonder. I realize it is because of fear.

God is going to get fear out of Abram. He was teaching Abram to trust God, and God does because he was able to say this when Abram went up on the mountain to sacrifice his son.

Genesis 22:8–9

> [8]And Abraham said, "My son, God will provide himself a lamb for a burnt offering": so they went both of them together. [9]And they came to the place which God had told him of; and Abraham built an altar there, and laid the wood in order, and bound Isaac his son, and laid him on the altar upon the wood.

I understand now that Abram could not have done that in the beginning when he first started walking with God, but now Abraham could do it.

God did this to teach him to trust in his word to obey him because he learned God was for him.

God trained him to trust him no matter what. It took a while, but he was not the same now. Just like Jonah was not the same after God was done teaching him because he wrote that book in the third person to let the reader know the Jonah who drafted the story of Jonah and him are not the same anymore.

2 Corinthians 5:17, "Therefore if any man be in Christ, he is a new creature: old things are passed away; behold, all things are become new."

God was doing the work; Abram did not know it at the time; Jonah did not know at the time; I did not know at the time, but I do now.

God is truly gentle, not just to his children but his enemy as well.

Genesis 4:7, "If thou do well, shalt thou not be accepted? and if thou does not well, sin lieth at the door. And unto thee shall be his desire, and thou shalt rule over him.

When God made this statement, he already knew Cain would kill Abel, but God, as I have learned, is so peaceful, kind, gentle, slow to anger, and full of love that he was trying to reason with him. He tried to reason a lot before he has to exercise his judgment.

Isaiah 1:18, "'Come now, and let us reason together,' saith the LORD: though your sins be as scarlet, they shall be as white as snow; though they be red like crimson, they shall be as wool."

What a statement.

God is holy, righteous, powerful, and just to all humankind.

King David knew also that God weigh out casualty to any judgment.

2 Samuel 24:12–14

> [12]Go and say unto David, thus saith the LORD, I offer thee three things; choose thee one of them, that I may do it unto thee. [13]So Gad came to David, and told him, and said unto him, shall seven years of famine come unto thee in thy land? or wilt thou flee three months before thine enemies, while they pursue thee? or that there be three days' pestilence in thy land? now advise, and see what answer I shall return to him that sent me. [14]And David said unto Gad, I am in a

great strait: let us fall now into the hand of the Lord; for his mercies are great: and let me not fall into the hand of man.

King David is a man after God's heart according to 1 Samuel 13:14. "But now thy kingdom shall not continue: the Lord hath sought him a man after his own heart, and the Lord hath commanded him to be captain over his people, because thou hast not kept that which the Lord commanded thee."

Acts 13:22, "And when he had removed him, he raised up unto them David to be their king; to whom also he gave their testimony, and said, I have found David the son of Jesse, a man after mine own heart, which shall fulfil all my will."

This shows that God is not a respecter of person, for God was willing to punish King David, a man after his own heart, and even Moses when he disobeyed God.

Numbers 20:12, "And the Lord spoke unto Moses and Aaron, Because ye believed me not, to sanctify me in the eyes of the children of Israel, therefore ye shall not bring this congregation into the land which I have given them."

I look at these two great men of God and how their punishment was not held back because of who they were. This shows even more of God's character.

I am deeply thankful of a God I can trust.

This is the God who will cause the flood on the earth and give instruction on how to build a boat to a man and his household. And the rest of life will perish in the flood.

This is the God that is going to cause the tribulation and the worst catastrophe in world history.

God is not only compassion, tenderness, love, benevolence, mercy, long-suffering, forbearance, and quick to forgive; he is so much more. Regardless of what some may believe, I am convinced that God is 100 percent involved in this world. Let us look at some scriptures that convince me.

Genesis 6:12, "And God looked upon the earth, and, behold, it was corrupt; for all flesh had corrupted his way upon the earth."

This I know, 1,600 years had passed since the creation of Adam and Eve. The patience and self-control that is seen here of God is remarkable.

2 Chronicles 18:19–22

> [19]And the Lord said, who shall entice Ahab king of Israel, that he may go up and fall at Ramothgilead? And one spoke saying after this manner, and another saying after that manner. [20]Then there came out a spirit, and stood before the Lord, and said, I will entice him. And the Lord said unto him, wherewith? [21]And he said, I will go out, and be a lying spirit in the mouth of all his prophets. And the Lord said, thou shalt entice him, and thou shalt also prevail: go out, and do even so. [22]Now therefore, behold, the Lord hath put a lying spirit in the mouth of these thy prophets, and the Lord hath spoken evil against thee.

This is one of the events recorded in the Scriptures that take me into the spirit world. I learned that there is noting that happens in the flesh world. That does not start in the spirit world. The spirit world discusses what they want done in the flesh world and then is carried out to be done. With two leaders one being God and the other being Satan instructing those under them for different assignment.

Job 1:6–8 "[6]Now there was a day when the sons of God came to present themselves before the Lord, and Satan came also among them. [7]And the Lord said unto Satan, whence comes thou? Then Satan answered the Lord, and said, from going to and fro in the earth, and from walking up and down in it. [8]And the Lord said unto Satan, Hast thou considered my servant Job, that there is none like him in the earth, a perfect and an upright man, one that feared God, and eschewed evil?"

Here I can see Satan in the spirit world as well. And again there is a conversation in the spirit world between Satan and God that is going to affect Job in the flesh world. God is bragging on Job, and he is not going to do nothing himself to Job but is going to allow it.

2 Chronicles 16:9 "For the eyes of the Lord run to and fro throughout the whole earth, to shew himself strong in the behalf of them whose heart is perfect toward him. Herein thou hast done foolishly: therefore from henceforth thou shalt have wars."

No doubt that God is not just involved. He knows everything going on. He will act when needed.

I can see it all throughout the scriptures. How God is looking and watching over not only his people, but also Satan and wicked people, especially those Satan is using.

I understand more than ever how in control God really is. With this knowledge concerning the days of Noah and the days that are coming in my time, he did not act quickly on the days of Noah, but had patience till the appointed time; in my time also, but he is still being patient.

God righteous fruits and control is very much established. Now we are going to look at his ability to know the beginning and ending and all in between.

Jonah 1:17 "Now the Lord had prepared a great fish to swallow up Jonah. And Jonah was in the belly of the fish three days and three nights."

With Jonah's rebellion, God already knew the event was going to happen before it ever did. Before God created the heavens and earth, he knew everything that would take place from beginning to end, even the Fall of humankind and the rebellion of Satan and his followers of angels, all the prophecies that have come to pass, which is knowing the future events.

Now that I know this about God, I am going to look at the comparison between the days of Noah and the things to come in my days.

God created heaven and earth and saw it was good. He was pleased with his work.

Genesis 1:31, "And God saw everything that he had made, and, behold, it was very good. And the evening and the morning were the sixth day."

Then this happens. Genesis 3:14–17 "¹⁴And the Lord God said unto the serpent, because thou hast done this, thou art cursed above all cattle, and above every beast of the field; upon thy belly shalt thou go, and dust shalt thou eat all the days of thy life: ¹⁵And I will put enmity between thee and the woman, and between thy seed and her seed; it shall bruise thy head, and thou shalt bruise his heel. ¹⁶Unto the woman he said, I will greatly multiply thy sorrow and thy conception; in sorrow thou shalt bring forth children; and thy desire shall be to thy husband, and he shall rule over thee. ¹⁷And unto Adam he said, because thou hast hearkened unto the voice of thy wife, and hast eaten of the tree, of which I commanded thee, saying, thou shalt not eat of it: cursed is the ground for thy sake; in sorrow shalt thou eat of it all the days of thy life."

The Fall of man brought sin into creation, and man's soul died, but as I have learned, everything starts in the spirit world before it gets to the flesh world.

Isaiah 14:12–14 "¹²How art thou fallen from heaven, O Lucifer, son of the morning! how art thou cut down to the ground, which didst weaken the nations! ¹³For thou hast said in thine heart, I will ascend into heaven, I will exalt my throne above the stars of God: I will sit also upon the mount of the congregation, in the sides of the north: ¹⁴I will ascend above the heights of the clouds; I will be like the most High."

Ezekiel 28:15, "Thou wast perfect in thy ways from the day that thou wast created, till iniquity was found in thee."

Sin started in heaven, then it went to the flesh world by Satan deceiving Eve, and from Eve to Adam. The war begins in heaven, but God will finish it on earth.

God's love for his creation is strong; he forms the first sacrifice in Genesis 3:21, "Unto Adam also and to his wife did the Lord God make coats of skins and clothed them."

God also forms the last sacrifice. Matthew 27:50, "Jesus, when he had cried again with a loud voice, yielded up the ghost."

This is how far God's love for his creation will go.

John 3:16, "For God so loved the world, that he gave his only begotten Son, that whosoever believeth in him should not perish, but have everlasting life."

I wanted to know what God meant when he said in Matthew 24:37, "But as the days of No'e were, so shall also the coming of the Son of man be."

My Heavenly Father started revealing a lot to me. I read this scripture: Isaiah 55:8–9, "8For my thoughts are not your thoughts, neither are your ways my ways, saith the Lord. 9For as the heavens are higher than the earth, so are my ways higher than your ways, and my thoughts than your thoughts."

I realize when God said my way are not his way or my thought are not his thought. He said they were not. To me that means they could be because he did not say they could not be. I just needed to ask for my thoughts be his thoughts and his way be my way. Then I remember this: James 4:2–3: 2Ye lust, and have not: ye kill, and desire to have, and cannot obtain: ye fight and war, yet ye have not, because ye ask not. 3Ye ask, and receive not, because ye ask amiss, that ye may consume it upon your lusts.

I started asking in the name of Jesus. God started revealing especially when I started applying this scripture: Matthew 6:33, "But seek ye first the kingdom of God, and his righteousness; and all these things shall be added unto you."

This is how generous God is when I do according to his guidelines. How awesome the things God has shown me since I have been seeking and asking with a better understanding.

I got to look at the people and what God was seeing in the days of Noah, to understand what has brought him to the point of destroying the world and what is coming in my present time, the tribulation.

Genesis 6:1–4 "1And it came to pass, when men began to multiply on the face of the earth, and daughters were born unto them, 2That the sons of God saw the daughters of men that they were fair; and they took them wives of all which they chose. 3And the Lord said, My spirit shall not always strive with man, for that he also is flesh: yet his days shall be an hundred and twenty years. ⁴There were giants in the earth in those days; and also after that, when the sons of God came in unto the daughters of men, and they bear children to them, the same became mighty men which were of old, men of renown."

When I am looking at these scriptures, words started standing out at me: (a) sons of God, (b) daughters, and (c) men.

The way I am seeing this, and my understanding is that these are three different groups.

Why would the Holy Spirit have the writer he inspires say sons of God saw the daughters of men were fair?

2 Peter 1:20–21, ²⁰"Knowing this first, that no prophecy of the scripture is of any private interpretation. ²¹For the prophecy came not in old time by the will of man: but holy men of God spake as they were moved by the Holy Ghost." This confirms that the Holy Ghost move on men to write the scriptures and not some private interpretation, so he worded it this way for a reason, because the sons of God is a different group from the daughters of men and man."

Job 2:1, "Again there was a day when the sons of God came to present themselves before the Lord, and Satan came also among them to present himself before the Lord."

Here I see it again, "sons of God" worded the same way as in Genesis. There is no denying it: these are angels, but when God talk about prophets he calls them son of man, like in Ezekiel 33:1–2: ¹"Again the word of the Lord came unto me, saying, ²Son of man, speak to the children of thy people, and say unto them, When I bring the sword upon a land, if the people of the land take a man of their coasts, and set him for their watchman."

God refers to his servant or prophets as sons of man.

Holy Ghost did this to help me understand that these are different groups.

John 1:12, "But as many as received him, to them gave he power to become the sons of God, even to them that believe on his name."

Humankind is not the sons of God, but sons of men. That way Jesus died so that humankind could become sons of God.

John 3:3, "Jesus answered and said unto him, Verily, verily, I say unto thee, Except a man be born again, he cannot see the kingdom of God."

Why would I need to be born again if am already a son of God? And I would not need to have the power to become the son of God. I have determined the sons of God in Genesis and Job are the first angels spoken of by Jude that left their first estate.

Jude 6, "And the angels which kept not their first estate, but left their own habitation, he hath reserved in everlasting chains under darkness unto the judgment of the great day."

Then I wonder how they could do that, and then I remember Hebrews.

Hebrews 13:1–2, "¹Let brotherly love continue. ²Be not forgetful to entertain strangers: for thereby some have entertained angels unawares."

This mean that angels could pull off looking like men to take the daughters of men for wives. This is a live portrait of what Absalom did to King David's concubines.

2 Samuel 16:22, "So they spread Absalom a tent upon the top of the house; and Absalom went in unto his father's concubines in the sight of all Israel."

These sons of God did this in front of all the host of heaven.

I knew it was not about man taking wives whom they desired to have, because throughout the scripture men have more than one wife, sometimes even a ridiculous number of wives.

1 Kings 11:3, "And he had seven hundred wives, princesses, and three hundred concubines: and his wives turned away his heart."

2 Chronicles 13:21, "But Abijah waxed mighty, and married fourteen wives, and begat twenty and two sons, and sixteen daughters."

My thought is Hebrew men did not want to sin against God's law.

Exodus 20:14, "Thou shalt not commit adultery."

The men of Hebrews found a loophole. They just married every woman they found attracted to or lusted for because there was no law that said there was a limit of wives you could marry. However, they could not commit adultery.

God even told David this. 2 Samuel 12:8, "And I gave thee thy master's house, and thy master's wives into thy bosom, and gave thee the house of Israel and of Judah; and if that had been too little, I would moreover have given unto thee such and such things."

God was not angry at him for having another wife. He was angry because of how he got her and how he did it.

God knew man would sin and expected it because he would not need to teach man to sacrifice.

Genesis 4:3–5 "³And in process of time it came to pass, that Cain brought of the fruit of the ground an offering unto the Lord. ⁴And Abel, he also brought of the firstlings of his flock and of the fat thereof. And the Lord had respect unto Abel and to his offering: ⁵But unto Cain and to his offering he had not respect. And Cain was very wroth, and his countenance fell."

These two men had sin and now had come to sacrifice before the Lord to get forgiveness, but one, God expected, the other he did not, because there is a right way and wrong way of pleasing God.

Luke 18:10–14 "¹⁰Two men went up into the temple to pray; the one a Pharisee, and the other a publican. ¹¹The Pharisee stood and prayed thus with himself, God, I thank thee, that I am not as other men are, extortioners, unjust, adulterers, or even as this publican. ¹²I fast twice in the week, I give tithes of all that I possess. ¹³And the publican, standing afar off, would not lift up so much as his eyes unto heaven, but smote upon his breast, saying, God be merciful to me a sinner. ¹⁴I tell you, this man went down to his house justified rather than the other: for every one that exalted himself shall be abased; and he that humbled himself shall be exalted."

I know in my time I no longer have to sacrifice as they did in the old covenant, but now I can go straight to him in prayer like these two gentlemen, but like Cain and Abel there is a right way and a wrong way, but the Pharisee was right about the publican. The publican even told God the same thing the Pharisee was telling God about all that was sinful about the publican, and he was all those things.

The Pharisee was a religious man doing everything that he thought would get him honor from God, but unfortunately for him the publican got respect like Abel did, but the Pharisee did not.

I learned just to be honest about my sins, fault, and failures, like this publican in which God did not hammer and judge him but rather had mercy and compassion on him as well as he will for me in my fault, failure, and sins. And he will help me overcome my fault, failure, and sin.

I am not saying keep committing sin but learn to do well. Some things are not as easy to overcome.

1 John 1:9 "If we confess our sins, he is faithful and just to forgive us our sins, and to cleanse us from all unrighteousness."

With all this in mind, what God was about to do in Noah's days, there is more to it because God was not just going to destroy all flesh on the earth over men marring the women they wanted when his chosen people, the Hebrews, would marry more than hundreds of women at a time and more in some cases are over sin that he made a temporarily fix, which is the sacrifice of sin offering, which is a picture of Jesus paying for my sins and the world's sins. I see that in the Book of Jonah with Nineveh and his thought on them. When God tells Jonah should he not be concern for all the souls in Nineveh and give them a chance even though they are wicked. This is why there was more to Noah's days for him to have to destroy the entire world.

Jonah 4:11, "And should not I spare Nineveh, that great city, wherein are more than sixscore thousand persons that cannot discern between their right hand and their left hand; and also much cattle?"

Then what was it? Let me see by going back to the serpent and his curse and understanding that Satan is using the serpent's body.

Genesis 3:14–15 "14And the Lord God said unto the serpent, because thou hast done this, thou art cursed above all cattle, and above every beast of the field; upon thy belly shalt thou go, and dust shalt thou eat all the days of thy life: 15And I will put enmity between thee and the woman, and between thy seed and her seed; it shall bruise thy head, and thou shalt bruise his heel."

God had seen what was going on. He knew he would have to act; why?

Luke 16:26, "And beside all this, between us and you there is a great gulf fixed: so that they which would pass from hence to you cannot; neither can they pass to us, that would come from thence."

Till Jesus the Son of God is sacrifice on the cross men's souls were not able to go back to God. These two places one torment the other paradise are where souls went because the permanent fix for humankind to be able to be present with God had not happened yet. Therefore, God put the temporarily fix in, just like this grace period that I am in to be saved I had to confess with my mouth and believe in my heart that Jesus paid for my sin with his death.

Romans 10:9–10 "9That if thou shalt confess with thy mouth the Lord Jesus, and shalt believe in thine heart that God hath raised him from the dead, thou shalt be saved. 10For with the heart man believeth unto righteousness; and with the mouth confession is made unto salvation."

In Noah's days you had to give of your best and first fruit as a sacrifice unto the Lord.

Satan knew this up to this point; in Noah's days it had been 1600 years for Satan to put in a plan to stop the woman's seed.

Satan knew he won the first battle, by tricking man into sinning, causing man to not be able to enter heaven, but a seed of a woman would fix man's mistake of listening to Satan. Satan knew God was saying a woman's child is going to destroy him, and he had to stop that child.

What would be the best way to do this? Satan is not stupid as for trying to stop God from stopping him, even though I know he loses. Satan is going to try to stop this child.

There was contamination of humankind by mixing angels' DNA with human DNA, causing a different bloodline. Satan would have won because there would not be a pure bloodline for God to use.

However, he failed; God knew what Satan was up to and stopped him, but it did not stop Satan from trying to stop the woman's seed.

I want to look at the attack on the woman's seed from Satan; I found it in the scriptures.

Exodus 1:16, "And he said, when ye do the office of a midwife to the Hebrew women and see them upon the stools; if it be a son, then ye shall kill him: but if it be a daughter, then she shall live."

Matthew 2:16 "Then Herod, when he saw that he was mocked of the wise men, was exceeding wroth, and sent forth, and slew all the children that were in Bethlehem, and in all the coasts thereof, from two years old and under, according to the time which he had diligently inquired of the wise men."

Matthew 4:5–6 "⁵Then the devil taketh him up into the holy city, and setteth him on a pinnacle of the temple, ⁶And saith unto him, if thou be the Son of God, cast thyself down: for it is written, He shall give his angels charge concerning thee: and in their hands they shall bear thee up, lest at any time thou dash thy foot against a stone."

Matthew 16:21–23 "²¹From that time forth began Jesus to shew unto his disciples, how that he must go unto Jerusalem, and suffer many things of the elders and chief priests and scribes, and be killed, and be raised again the third day. ²²Then Peter took him, and began to rebuke him, saying, be it far from thee, Lord: this shall not be unto thee. ²³But he turned, and said unto Peter, get thee behind me, Satan: thou art an offence unto me: for thou savourest not the things that be of God, but those that be of men."

Revelation 12:1–6 "¹And there appeared a great wonder in heaven; a woman clothed with the sun, and the moon under her feet, and upon her head a crown of twelve stars: ²And she being with child cried, travailing in birth, and pained to be delivered. ³And there appeared another wonder in heaven; and behold a great red dragon, having seven heads and ten horns, and seven crowns upon his heads. ⁴And his tail drew the third part of the stars of heaven and did cast them to the earth: and the dragon stood before the woman, which was ready to be delivered, for to devour her child as soon as it was born. ⁵And she brought forth a man child, who was to rule all nations with a rod of iron: and her child was caught up unto God, and to his throne. ⁶And the woman fled into the wilderness, where she hath a place prepared of God, that they should feed her there a thousand two hundred and threescore days."

Satan has been busy trying to stop this woman's seed all the way to the cross.

God loves his creation; he is doing and has done all he could to fix and repair what happened in the Garden of Eden. And he has accomplished it; now it is up to me whether I am going to do it the right way or the wrong way.

God is not going to destroy all flesh without a lot of patience and wisdom.

When I look at this scripture, I know I am right.

Matthew 13:27–30 "²⁷So the servants of the householder came and said unto him, Sir, didst not thou sow good seed in thy field? from whence then hath it tares? ²⁸He said unto them, an enemy hath done this. The servants said unto him, wilt thou then that we go and gather them up? ²⁹But he said, Nay; lest while ye gather up the tares, ye root up also the wheat with them. ³⁰Let both grow together until the harvest: and in the time of harvest, I will say to the reapers, Gather ye together first the tares, and bind them in bundles to burn them: but gather the wheat into my barn."

Satan is the enemy in this case and has been from the beginning of time.

God is not going to risk one person's life if he knows there's hope for him or her.

I want to get in God's mind and see what he was thinking when determining the destruction of all flesh in Noah's days.

Genesis 6:1–7 "¹And it came to pass, when men began to multiply on the face of the earth, and daughters were born unto them, ²That the sons of God saw the daughters of men that they were fair; and they took them wives of all which they chose. ³And the Lord said, my spirit shall not always strive with man, for that he also is flesh: yet his days shall be a hundred and twenty years. ⁴There were giants in the earth in those days; and also, after that, when the sons of God came in unto the daughters of men, and they bare children to them, the same became mighty men which were of old, men of renown. ⁵And God saw that the wickedness of man was great in the earth, and that every imagination of the thoughts of his heart was only evil continually. ⁶And it repented the Lord that he had made man on the earth, and it grieved him at his heart. ⁷And the Lord said, I will destroy man whom I have created from the face of the earth; both man, and beast, and the creeping thing, and the fowls of the air; for it repenteth me that I have made them."

When I read this and put in what I know about God's character, I conclude he was hurt. I think on the seventh days as he rested looking at his work and knowing it was good, he also knew what was coming; he knew he was going to have to repair a lot of damage caused by one of his created archangels.

Ezekiel 28:13 "Thou hast been in Eden the garden of God; every precious stone was thy covering, the sardius, topaz, and the diamond, the beryl, the onyx, and the jasper, the sapphire, the emerald, and the carbuncle, and gold: the workmanship of thy tabrets and of thy pipes was prepared in thee in the day that thou wast created."

God was hurt at what he was about to do. God love all his creation, heaven and earth. He created angels first and then humankind. Heaven sinned first with Satan; then earth sinned second due to Satan's deceiving Eve so that Adam would follow Eve in her disobedience.

The reason he regretted making humankind was he knew where those souls were going. Had they not been created, they would not have had to suffer for eternity. The wickedness of man had gotten to the point they stop sacrificing and seeking God, and they were doing ungodly thing to the point God had no choice.

I understand why God had to do what he did in Noah's days. He is going to do the same thing in my time but not with a flood; everything God is doing is because of the war Satan declared on him. And it effects on humankind.

Isaiah 14:13–14 "[13]For thou hast said in thine heart, I will ascend into heaven, I will exalt my throne above the stars of God: I will sit also upon the mount of the congregation, in the sides of the north: [14]I will ascend above the heights of the clouds; I will be like the most High."

Therefore, God says our fight is not with flesh and bones.

Ephesians 6:12, "For we wrestle not against flesh and blood, but against principalities, against powers, against the rulers of the darkness of this world, against spiritual wickedness in high places."

I came to understand that it is like a chess game.

God and Satan are the players. Earth and humankind are the game board and pieces.

Each player is trying to predict the other player's move. The more a player anticipates the other player's next move as far ahead as he can, the larger the advantage he has on the other player.

God will always have that advantage, and Satan never will; that is his problem and why he can never win against God; he will not build his throne above God's throne.

God is omnipotent and is everywhere at the same time. He is in the past, present, and future at the same time.

Revelation 4:8 "And the four beasts had each of them six wings about him; and they were full of eyes within: and they rest not day and night, saying, Holy, holy, holy, Lord God Almighty, which was, and is, and is to come."

Isaiah 14:26, "This is the purpose that is purposed upon the whole earth: and this is the hand that is stretched out upon all the nations."

Jeremiah 23:23–24 "23Am I a God at hand, saith the Lord, and not a God afar off? 24Can any hide himself in secret places that I shall not see him? saith the Lord. Do not I fill heaven and earth? saith the Lord."

God is like a seasoned professional playing a game of chess with a child with no chance to win, but the game pieces are real, live people, and the board is the earth.

The game pieces are made up of a king, a queen, knights, rooks, bishops, and pawns. There are two sets, one set is white and the other set black, to be able to tell them apart. White are God's pieces, and the black are Satan's pieces.

It is the fight between good and evil. Each set that belongs to them is their children to do as they please, and they can sacrifice any pieces at any time for their benefit. I see it in chess a lot; a player will even sacrifice their queen if need be.

That is why the scripture says this.

1 John 4:1, "Beloved, believe not every spirit, but try the spirits whether they are of God: because many false prophets are gone out into the world."

1 Kings 22:21–23 "21And there came forth a spirit, and stood before the Lord, and said, I will persuade him. 22And the Lord said unto him, wherewith? And he said, "I will go forth, and I will be a lying spirit in the mouth of all his prophets. And he said, thou shalt persuade him, and prevail also: go forth, and do so. 23Now therefore, behold, the Lord

hath put a lying spirit in the mouth of all these thy prophets, and the Lord hath spoken evil concerning thee.

My Lord impresses a question on me. He asks, Who is controlling the puppet? The puppet master, the strings, or the puppet itself?

I thought about it and decided it was the strings. If the strings are cut, the puppet could not move, and the puppet master could not make him move.

The puppet masters are the spirits, the strings are the emotions of the individual, and the puppet is the individual.

What I was learning was, if I cut the right string on the right emotion, the spirits could not make me give in to their purpose of why they are moving on me.

I also learned that these strings got to be cut with the Word of God.

Ephesians 6:17, "And take the helmet of salvation, and the sword of the Spirit, which is the word of God."

Hebrews 4:12–13 "[12]For the word of God is quick, and powerful, and sharper than any two-edged sword, piercing even to the dividing asunder of soul and spirit, and of the joints and marrow, and is a discerner of the thoughts and intents of the heart. [13]Neither is there any creature that "is not manifest in his sight: but all things are naked and opened unto the eyes of him with whom we have to do.

This is how I learned to use what God is teaching me. I would take an issue such as complaining; for me to cut that string I went to 1 Thessalonians 5:18, "In everything give thanks: for this is the will of God in Christ Jesus concerning you," and also Ephesians 5:20. God desires me to be thankful; if a spirit is moving on me trying to control my actions, this is what I learn to do and cut the string. Same way with anger; I hunt the scripture for anger, lust, and other emotions that can be cut with the Word of God because I have learned this is how the spirit world works to cause me to act out or anyone at any time to act out as well; therefore, it is important to learn to cut the strings.

A good example of humankind being puppets and game pieces is in these scripture.

Matthew 16:22–23 "²²Then Peter took him, and began to rebuke him, saying, be it far from thee, Lord: this shall not be unto thee. ²³But he turned, and said unto Peter, get thee behind me, Satan: thou art an offence unto me: for thou savourest not the things that be of God, but those that be of men."

1 Kings 22:22 "And the Lord said unto him, wherewith? And he said, I will go forth, and I will be a lying spirit in the mouth of all his prophets. And he said, thou shalt persuade him, and prevail also: go forth, and do so."

I learned that my battle is in my mind, where the spirits work to control the individual. This is how they can play the game with human lives.

When God goes to move a piece, it would look like this.

Jonah 1:1–2 "¹Now the word of the Lord came unto Jonah the son of Amittai, saying, ²Arise, go to Nineveh, that great city, and cry against it; for their wickedness is come up before me."

Here God is moving the game piece Jonah to go to a nation, but Satan would look like Matthew 2:16. "Then Herod, when he saw that he was mocked of the wise men, was exceeding wroth, and sent forth, and slew all the children that were in Bethlehem, and in all the coasts thereof, from two years old and under, according to the time which he had diligently inquired of the wise men."

Herod thinks he is doing this for his desire, which he is, but Satan is using him to get what he wants, Jesus dead.

Satan has been trying to stop this seed of a woman ever since he got cursed in the Garden of Eden by God.

This takes me back to the start of this book: why God is going to destroy all flesh on dry land. There is a war going on in the invisible world, between God and Satan. They both is building a kingdom. One in heaven, the other on earth. They both got their followers; they both use humankind as puppets. The more I get in the Word of God, the more I can see it with the Holy Ghost's help.

The difference is God loves his creation and the world; he is doing what is needed to save us.

Satan is doing it for himself and does not care whom he hurt, as the Scriptures say about him.

1 Peter 5:8, "Be sober, be vigilant; because your adversary the devil, as a roaring lion, walketh about, seeking whom he may devour."

Satan is not trying to stop the seed of the woman now, because he lost that battle at Calvary, but in Noah's days and up to the New Testament before Jesus died, he was trying to win the battle through contamination of DNA, taken out Israel, and stopping Jesus before he gets to the cross of Calvary, but when Jesus died on that cross, he paid the biggest debt that was ever owed in the history of humankind, because the Scriptures say this about the debt.

Romans 6:23, "For the wages of sin is death; but the gift of God is eternal life through Jesus Christ our Lord."

The only thing Satan can do now is cause one to disbelieve, doubt, and work against the word of God and the Holy Spirit. That is all Satan can do in this time I am living.

I got the Word of God, which is a lamp illuminating my path. Everything in the Bible can help me understand a lot with the help of the Holy Ghost.

Psalms 119:105, "Thy word is a lamp unto my feet, and a light unto my path."

2 Timothy 3:16, "All scripture is given by inspiration of God, and is profitable for doctrine, for reproof, for correction, for instruction in righteousness."

1 John 2:27 "But the anointing which ye have received of him abideth in you, and ye need not that any man teaches you: but as the same

anointing teacheth you of all things, and is truth, and is no lie, and even as it hath taught you, ye shall abide in him."

As in the days of Noah, Satan was doing damage trying to prevent God from accomplishing his promise, to restore man's relationship with God and his creation, but thank God he was not able, and the victory has already come through the seed of the woman he so much tried to stop: Jesus Christ, the Son of God, who takes away the sins of the world.

John 1:29, "The next day John seeth Jesus coming unto him, and saith, Behold the Lamb of God, which taketh away the sin of the world."

John 19:30, "When Jesus therefore had received the vinegar, he said, it is finished: and he bowed his head, and gave up the ghost."

I am so thankful for this understanding of God and his character, and knowing God loves his creation that had he not interfered in Noah's days and spotted Noah to preserve humankind and other creatures and stop the contamination of human DNA, Satan would have won, but thank God Satan did not and could not have won this battle for our salvation. The wages of sin have been paid for in full; only disbelief can stop an individual from salvation now.

Satan knows this, and this is how Satan battles now. If Satan can convince the world that God, Jesus, the Holy Spirit, the Word of God, aka the Bible, or any truth of God are not true or real, then he will be victorious.

What saddens me is that everyone's sin has been paid, which is death, and that wages have been paid for by the death of Jesus.

This is why Satan fought so hard to stop the seed of Eve. This is why Matthew's record of Jesus's family tree can be traced back to Eve. The seed God cursed Satan with could not be any other DNA. There is no one in hell for their sins; they are there because of unbelief.

In Noah's days God gave that generation and the generations all the way back to Adam's generation instruction on how and what to do: please him or stay right in fellowship with God.

My generation or this grace period I am in that started at Jesus's death have instruction on how to be in right fellowship, be born-again, how to escape the destruction coming, and how to become sons and daughters of God. What we have in common with Noah's days is there is God looking on our grace period to see who is going to be saved from the destruction that is coming to earth like he did in Noah's days.

During Noah's days it was him and his household, because God saw righteousness in him, which was faithfulness in keeping with the tradition taught by God to Adam to Noah in keeping the sacrifice.

God is looking for the same thing in my days as well: righteous people, which none is righteous, no, not one.

God is looking for Jesus's righteousness in his people to save from the destruction coming just like in Noah's days.

As in the days of Noah, God is looking at the wheat and tares. Tares to damnation, wheat to paradise.

CHAPTER 2

NOAH

Matthew 22:14, "For many are called, but few are chosen."

This is the case for my time or my grace period that I am in, but not so for Noah in his days.

Genesis 6:8, "But Noah found grace in the eyes of the Lord."

Genesis 6:8–9, 8"But Noah found grace in the eyes of the Lord. 9These are the generations of Noah: Noah was a just man and perfect in his generations, and Noah walked with God."

"In his generations" stands out to me, because when I study the generations, I learn God does not view each generation separately or independently. There can be up to three or even four generations together, depending on the length of life, that is, great-great-grandfather, great-grandfather, grandfather, father, and son, to witness each event of every generation except what is recorded in the Scriptures or what is written in the books that record in heaven on every soul that ever lived, but in my generation I can see what happened in Noah's generations and other generations to be able to compare with different generations with the help of the Holy Spirit to help me in my generation to understand the way I should live and what is coming in the future of other generations.

Exodus 1:6, "And Joseph died, and all his brethren, and all that generation."

Exodus 1:8, "Now there arose up a new king over Egypt, which knew not Joseph."

I noticed that all that happened in Joseph's days was all forgotten when the new king took power and brought hard times on the Hebrew's children. This is a good example of what happened in Noah's days.

The very first generation sinned against God.

Adam and Eve were taught how to please God, by forming the first sacrifice in their generation.

Genesis 3:21, "Unto Adam also and to his wife did the Lord God make coats of skins and clothed them."

And they instructed their children, Cain and Abel, which I can see in their effort that they were trained to sacrifice unto the Lord, but God wanted it his way, not an individual way. This is why Cain was not accepted.

Genesis 4:5, "But unto Cain and to his offering he had no respect. And Cain was very worth, and his countenance fell."

God was about to bring on destruction in Noah's days, but God found grace in his eyes, meaning he saw something about Noah. Let us look at what the Scriptures say about God and the generations.

This brings me back to Noah and his generations and how God chose Noah and his household out of all his generations. Let me look again at what God said about Noah.

Genesis 6:9, "These are the generations of Noah: Noah was a just man and perfect in his generations, and Noah walked with God."

Noah was not sinless, but he was doing what pleases God, like Abel did in his generation. Just off the top I realized I got to please God in my days, that pleasing God is the way to be able to escape the destruction coming one day in the future in some generation; but If I go to the grave, it is the same: I must be living by the way God has required of me, like Noah, who was a just a man, perfect in his generation, and walked with God.

Noah did not have a Bible, a temple, a denomination, or a church. I am not saying these things to put them down; I am just reminding myself what was in his generation that made him perfect. I believe what God said to Cain explains it.

Genesis 4:7, "If thou does well, shalt thou not be accepted? and if thou does' not well, sin lieth at the door. And unto thee shall be his desire, and thou shalt rule over him.

In other words, Noah was doing like Abel in his generation to please God.

Genesis 4:4, "And Abel, he also brought of the firstlings of his flock and of the fat thereof. And the Lord had respect unto Abel and to his offering."

Looking at Cain and Abel, now I know how God viewed them and what he expected of them; this also showed me how God viewed Noah and everyone else in his days.

All these people in Noah's days had 1,656 years from Adam and Eve's generation to get away from pleasing, trusting, believing, and walking with God, except Noah and his household.

Noah was a just man and perfect in his generations, and Noah walked with God.

Cain and Abel were trained from youth to the day that they were recorded in the scripture.

Noah was trained the same way from youth to where he is in his day when God called him.

God calling Noah takes me back to Matthew 22:14, "For many are called, but few are chosen."

Noah was the only one called out of everyone in his days, and because of his call his household was saved as well. This reminds me of what Paul said in Acts 16:31, "And they said, believe on the Lord Jesus Christ, and thou shalt be saved, and thy house, but in my time, many are saved few are chosen." Just like with the last plaque in Egypt.

Exodus 12:3, "Speak ye unto all the congregation of Israel, saying, In the tenth day of this month they shall take to them every man a lamb, according to the house of their fathers, a lamb for a house."

Exodus 12:7, "And they shall take of the blood and strike it on the two side posts and on the upper door post of the houses, wherein they shall eat it."

Exodus 12:23 "For the Lord will pass through to smite the Egyptians; and when he seeth the blood upon the lintel, and on the two side posts, the Lord will pass over the door, and will not suffer the destroyer to come in unto your houses to smite you."

The quality of the relationship between the head of the house and God in Noah's days is just as crucial in my time.

I also see another head of the household that is Jesus, the head of the body of Christ, or Church, when I look at Noah.

Jesus pleased his father, who is God, and his father God tells us this in Matthew 17:5 "While he yet spoke, behold, a bright cloud overshadowed them: and behold a voice out of the cloud, which said, this is my beloved Son, in whom I am well pleased; hear ye him."

Just as Noah was called to save humankind and not be destroyed with everyone else in his days, so was Jesus called to save the lost and just like Noah's household will be saved, those in Jesus's household will be saved from the destruction and death coming to all humankind in the grace period I live in.

Luke 19:10, "For the Son of man is come to seek and to save that which was lost."

Mark 3:35, "For whosoever shall do the will of God, the same is my brother, and my sister, and mother."

Romans 8:29, "For whom he did foreknow, he also did predestinate to be conformed to the image of his Son, that he might be the firstborn among many brethren."

What I also understand is I can see the parallel between Noah and his family being saved and Jesus and his family being saved.

I got to keep in mind that there was no old or new covenant from Adam's to Noah's time, just to sacrifice.

Noah and his household will be saved, and this is important because Noah is the head of the house, because God said Noah found grace, was perfect in his generation, and walked with God; he did not mention his family in that statement, because he is the head and is reasonable for his family and household and the leader, so it applied to his family because of him being right with God.

Noah is the head of the family, so when he is making a sacrifice, he is making it for his household, like with Cain and Abel.

I was thinking about Cain and Abel, with the thought of them being the head of each of their households. Cain is the head of his household and his sacrifice, as well as Abel's sacrifice, is very important, because their sacrifice is not just for them as individuals, but for their entire households, so when Cain is doing the sacrifice and God has no respect toward it, that means that Cain's household is not covered as well, so the rejection of Cain is God's rejection of his household; on the other hand, the acceptance of Abel's sacrifice from God is also accepting his entire family.

Job 1:5, "And it was so, when the days of their feasting were gone about, that Job sent and sanctified them, and rose up early in the morning, and offered burnt offerings according to the number of them."

Job said, "It may be that my sons have sinned and cursed God in their hearts." Thus did Job continually.

This is the love of a father toward his household, who did not take chances on his household's relation with God. He continually does this; this tells me that Job was not lazy, because a lot goes into sacrificing for his household, so I could only imagine if he did not have that heart with this knowledge. I know what was coming to him and his household later. Job had no idea what was going on behind the invisible world toward him and his household, but he knew what was acceptable to God.

Job 1:8, "And the Lord said unto Satan, Hast thou considered my servant Job, that there is none like him in the earth, a perfect and an upright man, one that feareth God, and escheweth evil?"

This sounds a lot like what God said in Noah's days.

Genesis 6:8–9, [8]"But Noah found grace in the eyes of the Lord. [9]These are the generations of Noah."

When I compare these two men together, I can see how God never changes. I can see why God saved Noah and bragged on Job, because regardless of what everyone else was doing in Noah's days, Noah seem to be the only one that was doing right, same as Job, which was sacrifice, putting God first, being just, and avoiding sin; I can also see why the rest perished, which would do the opposite of Noah, not sacrificing, walking away from God, embracing sin, and being evil continually.

Noah was not under any covenant, just what he was trained from youth, which started with God.

Noah had the knowledge of how to find grace and mercy with God to be saved from the destruction coming to all living things on dry land, but at the same time did not know he needed grace and mercy but was living and doing to his best ability to do everything he was taught as a child up to his present time.

This really made me think of what America's foundation is, what our nation, leaders, schools, churches, and parents would teach their youth up to adulthood, which is the freedom to worship, learn, please, and walk with God as an individual, group, family, and a nation without interference from the government or state.

To me the similarity is completely real in my heart, soul, and mind.

Here you got Adam and Eve being created, and I would go as far to say called of God, because we are all dead in ours sins till, we are called of God to repent and be born again, which is a new birth.

Ephesians 2:5, "Even when we were dead in sins, hath quickened us together with Christ, (by grace ye are saved)."

John 3:5–7 "⁵Jesus answered, Verily, verily, I say unto thee, except a man be born of water and of the Spirit, he cannot enter into the kingdom of God. ⁶That which is born of the flesh is flesh; and that which is born of the Spirit is spirit. ⁷Marvel not that I said unto thee, Ye must be born again."

I see how from Adam to Cain and Abel there is already rebellion against God, but Abel falls in line with Noah and Job.

Genesis 4:5, "But unto Cain and to his offering he had not respect. And Cain was very wroth, and his countenance fell."

From Cain and Abel to Noah to the present day the rebellion is even worse.

Genesis 6:5, "And God saw that the wickedness of man was great in the earth, and that every imagination of the thoughts of his heart was only evil continually."

Just using my nation, America, as an example, I look at her beginning how she started based on God's Word and knowledge of it and where we are as a nation now. To me it seems like generation from generation forget God and the history of important events. Here are some scriptures that remind and help me understand this.

Even a new king with record at hand did not remember Joseph and the great things he had done for Egypt and his father's house to save them from famine and how his God made this possible.

Exodus 1:8, "Now there arose up a new king over Egypt, which knew not Joseph."

Ezekiel 23:35, "Therefore thus saith the Lord God; Because thou hast forgotten me, and cast me behind thy back, therefore bear thou also thy lewdness and thy whoredoms."

Noah had not forgotten God.

I cannot help but remember Abraham and God having a conversation over how many righteous would it take to spare a nation. In Noah's case one, Noah himself, and being the head of his household spared them as well. That is something God showed me: that one righteous man availed much.

James 5:16, "Confess your faults one to another, and pray one for another, that ye may be healed. The effectual fervent prayer of a righteous man availeth much."

Genesis 18:23–32 "23And Abraham drew near, and said, wilt thou also destroy the righteous with the wicked? 24Peradventure there be fifty righteous within the city: wilt thou also destroy and not spare the place for the fifty righteous that are therein? 25That be far from thee to do after this manner, to slay the righteous with the wicked: and that the righteous should be as the wicked, that be far from thee: Shall not the Judge of all the earth do, right? 26And the Lord said, If I find in Sodom fifty righteous within the city, then I will spare all the place for their sakes. 27And Abraham answered and said, behold now, I have taken upon me to speak unto the Lord, which am but dust and ashes: 28Peradventure there shall lack five of the fifty righteous: wilt thou destroy all the city for lack of five? And he said, If I find there forty and five, I will not destroy it. 29And he spake unto him yet again, and said, Peradventure there shall be forty found there. And he said, I will not do it for forty's sake. 30And he said unto him, oh let not the Lord be angry, and I will speak Peradventure there shall thirty be found there. And he said, I will not do it, if I find thirty there. 31And he said, behold now, I have taken upon me to speak unto the Lord: Peradventure there shall be twenty found there. And he said, I will not destroy it for twenty's sake. 32And he said, oh let not the Lord be angry, and I will speak yet but this once: Peradventure ten shall be found there. And he said, I will not destroy it for ten's sake."

Noah, Abraham, and their faith, and everyone covered with the blood of Christ Jesus is considered righteous.

Why are these things so important to me? Because in my present time it is as in the days of Noah before the God told Noah of the destruction to come; he was living his life with his family regardless of the evil and madness around him.

This speaks volumes to me on how I should live my life during my present days as though I did not know destruction was coming, but I do, because before Noah knew, his life was accepted by God.

I cannot help but think of all I have at my disposal to learn, know, and be as close to God as possible, as in Noah's days he had the instructions that were handed down to him, by generation from generation and God speaking to him when he needed, so Noah knew of the danger coming and to build and ark with instruction.

I have the mouth of God, or Bible; I like to use the mouth of God myself because when I pick up the Bible the front cover and back cover is God's upper and lower lips, and all the pages in between is God's tongue speaking to me as he sees fit too.

Matthew 4:4, "But he answered and said, it is written, Man shall not live by bread alone, but by every word that proceeded out of the mouth of God."

Deuteronomy 8:3 "And he humbled thee, and suffered thee to hunger, and fed thee with manna, which thou knewest not, neither did thy fathers know; that he might make thee know that man doth not live by bread only, but by every word that proceedeth out of the mouth of the Lord doth man live."

I am blessed to be living in these days of mine and have this Bible to tell me how I should live.

Noah did not have this advantage, but God had been planning for the word of God as well as his son Jesus to be formed and one being my salvation and the other my instruction. I do not have sacrifice the way Noah did in his days.

The fix was to prepare a sacrifice and cover sin in Noah days, but the problem was it cannot be permanent; it was a temporary fix. This is why it continues over and over.

My sacrifice was made at Golgotha, and this is a permanent fix.

In Noah's days they worked for salvation as for preparing the sacrifice to the repentant.

My Father in heaven prepared me and not me alone, but the greatest sacrifice ever for the whole world that would pay the wages of sin I owed, by sacrificing his only begotten son, Jesus Christ.

I am not working for salvation, for it is a gift, it is free, but I did have to accept the gift by grace through faith. Romans 6:23, "For the wages of sin is death; but the gift of God is eternal life through Jesus Christ our Lord."

John 1:29, "The next day John seeth Jesus coming unto him, and saith, Behold the Lamb of God, which taketh away the sin of the world."

Ephesians 2:8–9, [8]"For by grace are ye saved through faith; and that not of yourselves: it is the gift of God: [9]Not of works, lest any man should boast."

John 3:16, "For God so loved the world, that he gave his only begotten Son, that whosoever believeth in him should not perish, but have everlasting life."

Matthew 17:5, "While he yet spake, behold, a bright cloud overshadowed them: and behold a voice out of the cloud, which said, this is my beloved Son, in whom I am well pleased; hear ye him."

My sins have been paid in full. I have a Bible that instructs me, and Holy Ghost is in me who is the comforter or the Holy Spirit that moved upon men to write the Bible, so the author is in me and other born-again believers.

My Father got me to understand it this way; I have a locker, and in that locker is all the wealth, treasure, and wonder that is overflowing, but there a combination lock, and I need someone with the combination to unlock it, which is the Holy Spirit in me to unlock what he is ready for me to understand. He has shown a lot to me through the years.

2 Peter 1:21, "For the prophecy came not in old time by the will of man: but holy men of God spake as they were moved by the Holy Ghost."

John 16:7, "Nevertheless I tell you the truth; It is expedient for you that I go away: for if I go not away, the Comforter will not come unto you; but if I depart, I will send him unto you."

John 14:26, "But the Comforter, which is the Holy Ghost, whom the Father will send in my name, he shall teach you all things, and bring all things to your remembrance, whatsoever I have said unto you."

With all our technology, plenty of technology, computers, social media, we have all the information at our fingertips.

I can take what God put in my heart, google it, and have it put together on paper or a laptop file for when it is needed.

There is no reason that I cannot study except for laziness, with all I have at my disposal.

2 Timothy 2:15, "Study to shew thyself approved unto God, a workman that needeth not to be ashamed, rightly dividing the word of truth."

Proverbs 6:6–11 "⁶Go to the ant, thou sluggard; consider her ways, and be wise: ⁷Which having no guide, overseer, or ruler, ⁸Provideth her meat in the summer, and gathereth her food in the harvest. ⁹How long wilt thou sleep, O sluggard? When wilt thou arise out of thy sleep? ¹⁰Yet a little sleep, a little slumber, a little folding of the hands to sleep: ¹¹So shall thy poverty come as one that travelleth, and thy want as an armed man."

O sluggard, hit home with me, because my Father in heaven knows me and how lazy I can get. I have not been praying or reading the Bible as well as other things but found it easy to put off spiritual needs for foolish needs such as TV watching or playing Internet games for long periods of time if not all day, but I have now learned the importance of focusing on spiritual needs.

Peter, James, and John had to learn as well by what is said in Matthew 26:40, "And he cometh unto the disciples, and findeth them asleep, and saith unto Peter, what, could ye not watch with me one hour?"

Luke 21:36, "Watch ye therefore, and pray always, that ye may be accounted worthy to escape all these things that shall come to pass, and to stand before the Son of man."

Peter and the other disciples and I had to learn the importance of watching and praying because that is what God is looking for in his believers or born-again sons and daughters for my days now, but God was looking in Noah's days for someone he could save as well as other creatures of the land.

Noah was not lazy, because for Noah to get this grace and the attention from God he had to be doing what was required of him. I can only imagine what Noah and his household had to do to get God's favor with raising animals and preparing all that to sacrifice unto God. And the only instruction he had was what had been handed down to him from previous generations.

This is the importance to me of knowing there is a calling, from the time I am in and beyond my time, God is calling me and others to prepare for what is coming.

1 Thessalonians 4:17, "Then we which are alive and remain shall be caught up together with them in the clouds, to meet the Lord in the air: and so, shall we ever be with the Lord."

I know that these things are coming; Noah did not until he was told by God but still was carrying the tradition handed down to him. Rather, he was expecting the anointed one from the symbolism of the sacrifice that was a picture of Jesus coming and be sacrificed for our sins. He did not know the end was coming in his day or that his would be the only family to survive the end of the world; again, until God told him. All the corruption and wickedness going on around him did not stop Noah staying in a good relationship with God during his days.

This really makes me realize how important it is to not be lazy, but manage my time, studying the Word of God, and prayer better because I have no excuse for not being prepared for Jesus's return and if I missed that, the seven years of tribulation will be worst.

God has given me the Word of God, which not only tells me of the days of Noah but the Rapture and the seven years of tribulation and much more.

Noah was just living his life going about his everyday routine as to what he thought it was, with no more information than what was handed down to him. At least not as much information as I have in the Bible, through the Holy Spirit, plus Jesus paid my wages with his death so there is no more sacrifice needed for my sins; the debt has been paid in full. How much better I have it in my time than what Noah did, but what Noah and I both got that made a difference is God; he is who can save, protect, provide, and deliver.

Noah has been called and chosen from God to save humankind but not his generation: the future generations to come. As we know, he and his household are the only humans that will survive.

The same is true in the grace period that we are in, starting with Jesus's sacrifice for the sins of world, then the disciples he called to preach the grace and that sins have been paid for everyone to receive, and from the disciples to future believers, all the way to the last believer, which is the great calling always, the Rapture, and end of the grace period.

Just like Noah, God calls and chooses a person for a purpose that he wants that person to do.

Matthew 22:14, "For many are called, but few are chosen."

Romans 8:28, "And we know that all things work together for good to them that love God, to them who are the called according to his purpose."

Noah was called to build an ark, and many are called for different tasks.

Romans 12:4–8 "[4]For as we have many members in one body, and all members have not the same office: [5]So we, being many, are one body in Christ, and every one member one of another. [6]Having then gifts differing according to the grace that is given to us, whether prophecy, let us prophesy according to the proportion of faith; [7]Or ministry, let us wait on our ministering: or he that teaches, on teaching; [8]Or he that exhorteth, on exhortation: he that giveth, let him do it with simplicity; he that ruleth, with diligence; he that sheweth mercy, with cheerfulness."

Mark 16:15, "And he said unto them, go ye into all the world, and preach the gospel to every creature."

The parallel between Noah's days and the grace period of the present time is amazing once my Heavenly Father started revealing it.

Noah is a shadow of me or anyone else that has been called to be saved in this grace period from the wrath of God.

Just like Noah, I got to do what God says to do, so I do not perish like everyone else in Noah's days.

That is to believe in the Son Of God.

Acts 16:30–33 "³⁰And brought them out, and said, Sirs, what must I do to be saved? ³¹And they said, believe on the Lord Jesus Christ, and thou shalt be saved, and thy house. ³²And they spake unto him the word of the Lord, and to all that were in his house. ³³And he took them the same hour of the night, and washed their stripes; and was baptized, he and all his, straightway."

Mark 16:16, "He that believeth and is baptized shall be saved; but he that believeth not shall be damned."

It is a whole lot easier to believe that Jesus died for my sins than building an ark to save my soul, but Jesus took the hardest part that I could not or would not want to do, and that is to take upon himself the punishments, pain, humiliation, suffering, and finally death. All for me so I would not have to, and all I need is to believe in him. And he would do the work.

Philippians 1:6, "Being confident of this very thing, that he which hath begun a good work in you will perform it until the day of Jesus Christ."

Noah was to build the Ark in his days to be saved, but Jesus is the ark for me and the days I am in to be saved.

John 10:9, "I am the door: by me if any man enters in, he shall be saved, and shall go in and out, and find pasture."

Noah was not under the law; he was under the Adam covenant, which was where God did the first sacrifice for humankind after the Fall, and as I learned already, it was still being practiced up to the scene in the scripture with Abel and Cain in which Noah was still practicing the sacrifice before and after the flood. Before because God said he had seen righteousness in Noah that had to be him doing the sacrifice that represents Jesus coming and dying for humankind's sins, and after when Noah came off the Ark.

Genesis 7:1, "And the Lord said unto Noah, come thou and all thy house into the ark; for thee have I seen righteous before me in this generation."

Genesis 8:20, "And Noah builded an altar unto the Lord; and took of every clean beast, and of every clean fowl, and offered burnt offerings on the altar."

The parallel between the days of Noah and the grace period in our time concerning this thought is that we in this grace period from Jesus Christ's death and the Rapture are taken away are not under the law anymore once we receive Jesus Christ, so anyone who accepts and believes in the son of God is no longer under the law.

Romans 10:4, "For Christ is the end of the law for righteousness to everyone that believeth."

Romans 10:9, "That if thou shalt confess with thy mouth the Lord Jesus, and shalt believe in thine heart that God hath raised him from the dead, thou shalt be saved."

God is looking to save the world from the coming wrath both in Noah's days and in the grace period we are living in.

God is looking, as I know from earlier in this book, for grace and righteousness. That can only be found in Jesus who lives in his believers.

Genesis 6:8, "But Noah found grace in the eyes of the Lord."

Genesis 7:1, "And the Lord said unto Noah, come thou and all thy house into the ark; for thee have I seen righteous before me in this generation."

The same is what God is looking for in our days and the grace period we are in, but we humans are not righteous, no, not one, and humankind cannot keep the law; it condemned humankind.

Romans 3:10, "As it is written, there is none righteous, no, not one."

Psalms 53:1–3 "[1]The fool hath said in his heart, there is no God. Corrupt are they and have done abominable iniquity: there is none that doeth good. [2]God looked down from heaven upon the children of men, to see if there were any that did understand, that did seek God. [3]Every one of them is gone back: they are altogether become filthy; there is none that doeth good, no, not one."

Noah walks with God; this is another reason he was chosen. Genesis 6:9, "These are the generations of Noah: Noah was a just man and perfect in his generations, and Noah walked with God."

Walking with God to me is the same as fellowshipping with God or as praying without ceasing as it is said in 1 Thessalonians 5:17, "Pray without ceasing, because Noah walking with God, I could only imagine was awesome; like with Enoch walk with God and God took him."

Genesis 5:24, "And Enoch walked with God: and he was not; for God took him."

Enoch walks so close to God that they walked on up to glory to the throne of God.

Noah was doing the same thing; I know this because he could hear God's voice.

Elijah was walking so close to God that God sent him a ride to escort him to the throne of God as well.

2 Kings 2:1, "And it came to pass, when the Lord would take up Elijah into heaven by a whirlwind, that Elijah went with Elisha from Gilgal."

2 Kings 2:11, "And it came to pass, as they still went on, and talked, that, behold, there appeared a chariot of fire, and horses of fire, and parted them both asunder; and Elijah went up by a whirlwind into heaven."

Jonah walks with God so close that he knew God's voice and knew his character so much that he knows how God would react to Nineveh.

Jonah 4:2 "And he prayed unto the Lord, and said, I pray thee, O Lord, was not this my saying, when I was yet in my country? Therefore, I fled before unto Tarshish: for I knew that thou art a gracious God, and merciful, slow to anger, and of great kindness, and repentest thee of the evil."

I know that walking with God is very important because even in our days and this grace period we are in, the New Testament scriptures said to walk in him Christ Jesus.

Colossians 2:6, "As ye have therefore received Christ Jesus the Lord, so walk ye in him."

Walking with God was needed in Noah's days and is needed in this present grace period as well.

The three things I see are that both in Noah's days and in present time, we needed to find grace, righteousness, and walk with God.

Noah found grace by his obedience by keeping the sacrifice, and God was able to see righteousness in Noah because of what the sacrifice symbolizes, which is what we look back on and what Noah and his days look forward to, and that was the sacrifice of God's own son for the sins of the world. And walking with God in obedience, fellowship, and in repentance whenever we falter, fail, or flat-out sin; that is what their sacrifice was for.

This is also true in the days we live in; we need grace to be able to see righteousness in us and walk with God.

Ephesians 2:8, "For by grace are ye saved through faith; and that not of yourselves: it is the gift of God."

2 Corinthians 5:21, "For he hath made him to be sin for us, who knew no sin; that we might be made the righteousness of God in him."

Micah 6:8, "He hath shewed thee, O man, what is good; and what doth the Lord require of thee, but to do justly, and to love mercy, and to walk humbly with thy God?"

Galatians 5:16, "This I say then, walk in the Spirit, and ye shall not fulfil the lust of the flesh."

Romans 6:4, "Therefore we are buried with him by baptism into death: that like as Christ was raised up from the dead by the glory of the Father, even so we also should walk in newness of life."

What I have learned and been taught is to trust the Lord God and obey his words rather back in Noah's days, when he could hear the voice of the Lord; now in our days, or grace period in present time, one can hear his word or read his Word, but both actions come from his Word, trust and obey, and that is what Noah was able to do, and that's what is expected of us to do in this grace period. This is what is expected of all of God's people regardless of the Old Testament, the New Testament, or the present day; for example, when you look at the success of God's people this is what they all have in common.

2 Kings 18:5–7 "⁵He trusted in the Lord God of Israel; so that after him was none like him among all the kings of Judah, nor any that were before him. ⁶For he clave to the Lord, and departed not from following him, but kept his commandments, which the Lord commanded Moses. ⁷And the Lord was with him; and he prospered whithersoever he went forth: and he rebelled against the king of Assyria, and served him not."

Noah was also a picture of Jesus as said earlier in this chapter to save his household. And this is what God the Father had Jesus his Son to do for his family.

Noah's household needed to and should obey Noah for being spared or saved from the destruction that God said was coming, and this is what one have to do. And we know that there is an appointment in time for man to die or the Rapture, which will bring up the dead in Christ first and them that are alive afterward. Either way, I have to be ready for both while I go about my days and life like Noah did until given instructions on things that he would have me do, because he wants me to live a life that others can see that I am peculiar, just, generous, and anything else that bears the fruit of God, his character, and his way, and this is exactly what Noah was able to do in his days, and his days run parallel to my days.

2 Peter 3:7, "But the heavens and the earth, which are now, by the same word are kept in store, reserved unto fire against the day of judgment and perdition of ungodly men."

Malachi 4:1 "For, behold, the day cometh, that shall burn as an oven; and all the proud, yea, and all that do wickedly, shall be stubble: and the day that cometh shall burn them up, saith the Lord of hosts, that it shall leave them neither root nor branch."

Revelation 21:1, "And I saw a new heaven and a new earth: for the first heaven and the first earth were passed away; and there was no more sea."

When the Lord revealed to me how Noah's days and the grace period or the present time run so parallel to one another, I saw it was more than drinking and eating or being given in marriage.

God wanted me to look harder at the whole event and break it all down, to show everything from God choosing Noah and from Noah building the Ark to the rainbow being placed to be a reminder to God, and how all this shows the picture and the event of this grace and that it does run parallel to the events of Jesus's birth, his crucifixion, the Church, the Rapture, the bride of Christ, seven years of tribulation, the two witnesses, the coming up of the new Jerusalem; all of this was revealed to me, and I was to put it in a book.

As Peter said to the cripple man, silver and gold I have none, but what I have I will give you, which was healing and in Jesus's name made the lame man to walk. In my case, silver and gold I do not have, but what I do have I give you, which is the wisdom, knowledge, and understanding that God gave me, not that I am special, not that I am worthy, but simply because he chose me, and he wants me to do it. I am so honored and grateful that he chose me to do this.

Noah, I have come to understand, is a great man to study and to learn what God is expecting and looking for in me.

To recap, in Noah's days and present time, or as I call it, grace period, both Noah and I know there's destruction coming to humankind, and both know what we must do to be saved from the destruction that is coming.

Noah knew that no one would be saved but him and his household in his days, and I know that not everyone is going to be saved during the grace period we are in, even though God would not have any to be lost or perish.

Matthew 7:14, "Because strait is the gate, and narrow is the way, which leadeth unto life, and few there be that find it."

Matthew 7:21, "Not everyone that saith unto me, Lord, Lord, shall enter into the kingdom of heaven; but he that doeth the will of my Father which is in heaven."

2 Peter 3:9, "The Lord is not slack concerning his promise, as some men count slackness; but is longsuffering to us-ward, not willing that any should perish, but that all should come to repentance."

Noah had to believe God's word that he was going to destroy the earth with a flood and that he had to build a ship called the Ark for him and his household to be saved.

During the grace period in this present time has to be the same thing; I have to believe in what I must do to be ready, whether I go by grave or go by Rapture, and to do this I must know how to be saved during this grace period.

Romans 10:9–10 "⁹That if thou shalt confess with thy mouth the Lord Jesus, and shalt believe in thine heart that God hath raised him from the dead, thou shalt be saved. ¹⁰For with the heart man believeth unto righteousness; and with the mouth confession is made unto salvation."

Acts 16:30–31, "³⁰And brought them out, and said, Sirs, what must I do to be saved? ³¹And they said, believe on the Lord Jesus Christ, and thou shalt be saved, and thy house."

Noah was called to build this ship.

God in this grace period chosen souls to help build the kingdom of God.

1 Corinthians 7:17, "But as God hath distributed to every man, as the Lord hath called every one, so let him walk. And so, ordain I in all churches."

1 Peter 5:10, "But the God of all grace, who hath called us unto his eternal glory by Christ Jesus, after that ye have suffered a while, make you perfect, stablish, strengthen, settle you."

2 Timothy 1:9, "Who hath saved us, and called us with an holy calling, not according to our works, but according to his own purpose and grace, which was given us in Christ Jesus before the world began."

Mark 16:15–16, [15]"And he said unto them, Go ye into all the world, and preach the gospel to every creature. [16]He that believeth and is baptized shall be saved; but he that believeth not shall be damned."

Matthew 28:18–20 "[18]And Jesus came and spoke unto them, saying, All power is given unto me in heaven and in earth. [19]Go ye therefore, and teach all nations, baptizing them in the name of the Father, and of the Son, and of the Holy Ghost: [20]Teaching them to observe all things whatsoever I have commanded you: and, lo, I am with you always, even unto the end of the world. Amen."

This is it, just like Noah, God is in this present time is calling souls to be saved from destruction and do a job till God children are called home by grave or Rapture.

CHAPTER 3

THE BUILDING OF THE ARK

Philippians 2:12, "Wherefore, my beloved, as ye have always obeyed, not as in my presence only, but now much more in my absence, work out your own salvation with fear and trembling."

This is what Noah was about to do, work out his salvation with fear and trembling, because he knew what was coming and knew what he had to do, and that is to build his salvation and his household's salvation, which would be the Ark, by God's command and instruction.

Material of the Ark

Genesis 6:14, "Make thee an ark of gopher wood; rooms shalt thou make in the ark, and shalt pitch it within and without with pitch."

Gopher wood or tree is unknown nowadays, or some say it could be a cypress tree.

Dealing with the unknown tree reminds me of what Paul said to the very superstitious people, and he told them of this unknown God.

Acts 17:22–31

> [22]Then Paul stood in the midst of Mars' hill, and said, Ye men of Athens, I perceive that in all things ye are too superstitious. [23]For as I passed by, and beheld your devotions, I found an altar with this inscription, to the unknown God. Whom therefore ye ignorantly worship, him declare I unto you. [24]God that made the world and all things therein, seeing

that he is Lord of heaven and earth, dwelleth not in temples made with hands; [25]Neither is worshipped with men's hands, as though he needed anything, seeing he giveth to all life, and breath, and all things; [26]And hath made of one blood all nations of men for to dwell on all the face of the earth, and hath determined the times before appointed, and the bounds of their habitation; [27]That they should seek the Lord, if haply they might feel after him, and find him, though he be not far from every one of us: [28]For in him we live, and move, and have our being; as certain also of your own poets have said, For we are also his offspring. [29]Forasmuch then as we are the offspring of God, we ought not to think that the Godhead is like unto gold, or silver, or stone, graven by art and man's device. [30]And the times of this ignorance God winked at; but now commandeth all men everywhere to repent: [31]Because he hath appointed a day, in the which he will judge the world in righteousness by that man whom he hath ordained; whereof he hath given assurance unto all men, in that he hath raised him from the dead.

And just like the Ark, everyone in it lived and everyone outside the Ark died.

God today is unknown to many because their eyes are blind and not only that they are not able to believe there is a God and the devil with his agenda with the help of his dominions in high places not only wants to make sure he stays unknown, but they are getting anything that points to Christ Jesus either unlawful, banned, or destroyed, but I am thankful God is greater.

Ephesians 6:12, "For we wrestle not against flesh and blood, but against principalities, against powers, against the rulers of the darkness of this world, against spiritual wickedness in high places."

1 Peter 5:8, "Be sober, be vigilant; because your adversary the devil, as a roaring lion, walketh about, seeking whom he may devour."

1 John 4:4, "Ye are of God, little children, and have overcome them: because greater is he that is in you, than he that is in the world."

Some people think the Ark was made from cypress trees; if so, cypress is good for furniture, canoes, or other things because it is waterproof. Also, the tree itself does not change year-round unless damaged but is able to stay green year-round; not only is it great material when you cut it down to be used for whatever project is needed, but also the roots and the tree stump are a great source to start a fire because when it sets up for a long period of time, it turns into what most people call rich pine, and it is just as good as gasoline or kerosene for starting fires.

I like the thought of the cypress because it reminds me of Jesus Christ. From these scriptures.

Luke 3:16 "John answered, saying unto them all, I indeed baptize you with water; but one mightier than I cometh, the latchet of whose shoes I am not worthy to unloose: he shall baptize you with the Holy Ghost and with fire:"

Hebrews 13:8, "Jesus Christ is the same yesterday, and today, and forever."

1 Corinthians 3:9–11 "⁹For we are labourers together with God: ye are God's husbandry, ye are God's building. ¹⁰According to the grace of God, which is given unto me, as a wise master builder, I have laid the foundation, and another buildeth thereon. But let every man take heed how he buildeth thereupon. ¹¹For other foundation can no man lay than that is laid, which is Jesus Christ."

The pitch is what was used to seal in and out of the Ark when building or done building. This reminds me of the Holy Ghost. The Holy Ghost seal me on the inside and help me on the outside to let Jesus Christ and his righteousness be seen.

Ephesians 1:13, "In whom ye also trusted, after that ye heard the word of truth, the gospel of your salvation: in whom also after that ye believed, ye were sealed with that holy Spirit of promise."

Ephesians 4:30, "And grieve not the holy Spirit of God, whereby ye are sealed unto the day of redemption."

John 14:26, "But the Comforter, which is the Holy Ghost, whom the Father will send in my name, he shall teach you all things, and bring all things to your remembrance, whatsoever I have said unto you."

God is awesome; he can have multiple things going on in one scene like an onion; peel off the first layer, and God reveals to me that there are more layers yet to come in that one scene, because when I look at the material that is being used on the Ark, I cannot help notice how God even lets these things run parallel with things to come and the days that I am living in.

The trees that are used in building the Ark are very important because the trees are a picture of me and other born-again children of God in the days that I am living.

Trees in the scriptures sometimes refer to people.

Psalms 1:3, "And he shall be like a tree planted by the rivers of water, that bringeth forth his fruit in his season; his leaf also shall not wither; and whatsoever he doeth shall prosper."

Jeremiah 17:8 "For he shall be as a tree planted by the waters, and that spreadeth out her roots by the river, and shall not see when heat cometh, but her leaf shall be green; and shall not be careful in the year of drought, neither shall cease from yielding fruit."

Zechariah 4:11–14 "[11]Then answered I, and said unto him, what are these two olive trees upon the right side of the candlestick and upon the left side thereof? [12]And I answered again, and said unto him, What be these two olive branches which through the two golden pipes empty the golden oil out of themselves? [13]And he answered me and said, knowest thou not what these be? And I said, No, my lord. [14]Then said he, these are the two anointed ones, that stand by the Lord of the whole earth."

Luke 13:6–9 "[6]He spake also this parable; A certain man had a fig tree planted in his vineyard; and he came and sought fruit thereon, and found none. [7]Then said he unto the dresser of his vineyard, Behold, these three years I come seeking fruit on this fig tree, and find none: cut it down; why cumbereth it the ground? [8]And he answering said unto him, Lord, let it alone this year also, till I shall dig about it, and dung it: ⁹And if it bear fruit, well: and if not, then after that thou shalt cut it down."

Mark 8:24, "And he looked up, and said, I see men as trees, walking."

The Spirit of God was showing me how important is to understand this about the trees because it helps to see how it relates to the days we are in, and Noah's days and our days run parallel to each other.

First, I look at these trees, and know that they had to die and be transformed into the shape and fit in what every spot that it was being made for.

Noah is a picture of God, and God-chosen people or his born-again children's are a picture of a tree. He chose to die to self and to be made or formed into a piece of craftsmanship to work in his body, which he is building for his kingdom.

Noah's three sons are a picture of the Trinity working together building the Ark for salvation (the Father, Son, and Holy Ghost) to help the children of God, or born-again believers, to escape the destruction coming: the lake of fire and the seven-year tribulation.

The time it took to build the Ark, some studies show to be 55 to 75 years or maybe 120 years, but regardless of the time it took to build it, it was the only way to be saved from the coming destruction.

This would be their grace period, from the time they started to the door closed by God, in Noah's days, but it is a picture of the event coming and has come in my days.

Romans 6:8, "Now if we be dead with Christ, we believe that we shall also live with him."

Galatians 2:20, "I am crucified with Christ: nevertheless I live; yet not I, but Christ liveth in me: and the life which I now live in the flesh I live by the faith of the Son of God, who loved me, and gave himself for me."

Ephesians 4:22–24 "²²That ye put off concerning the former conversation the old man, which is corrupt according to the deceitful lusts; ²³And be renewed in the spirit of your mind; [24]And that ye put on the new man, which after God is created in righteousness and true holiness."

Luke 9:23, "And he said to them all, if any man will come after me, let him deny himself, and take up his cross daily, and follow me."

I realize that these trees did not go straight on the Ark until they were changed or transferred into the piece of wood for the part of the Ark it would be used for, so technically both Noah's days and the days we are living in are working out their salvation to the fear of the Lord.

Philippians 2:12–13 "[12]Wherefore, my beloved, as ye have always obeyed, not as in my presence only, but now much more in my absence, work out your own salvation with fear and trembling. [13]For it is God which worketh in you both to will and to do of his good pleasure."

Noah cut down trees to work on them to shape and form into a piece it needed to create an Ark.

God is calling people to die to self and fellowship with his Son Jesus to build the body of Christ.

The Ark and Jesus are both a picture of salvation.

The only difference is the Ark has already been built, but the body of Christ is being built as I draft this book.

1 Corinthians 12:12–13 "[12]For as the body is one, and hath many members, and all the members of that one body, being many, are one body: so also, is Christ. [13]For by one Spirit are we all baptized into one body, whether we be Jews or Gentiles, whether we be bond or free; and have been all made to drink into one Spirit."

1 Corinthians 12:27, "Now ye are the body of Christ, and members in particular."

Colossians 1:18, "And he is the head of the body, the church: who is the beginning, the firstborn from the dead; that in all things he might have the preeminence."

The Ark is one body, but there are many members of trees becoming the Ark. The same happens with the body of Christ: it is many born-again believers making up the body of Christ.

There has to be a starting point, the very first piece to start the building, both the Ark and the body of Christ. Each one is very important, the firstborn.

The first tree cut down to start the Ark is a picture of Jesus, the firstborn in the grace period I am living in, the cornerstone of the body of Christ. Every tree after the first tree is a picture of all the born-again believers from the start to finish of the Ark.

Ephesians 2:20–22 "20And are built upon the foundation of the apostles and prophets, Jesus Christ himself being the chief corner stone; 21In whom all the building fitly framed together groweth unto an holy temple in the Lord: 22In whom ye also are builded together for an habitation of God through the Spirit."

Psalms 118:22, "The stone which the builders refused is become the head stone of the corner."

Acts 4:10–12 "10Be it known unto you all, and to all the people of Israel, that by the name of Jesus Christ of Nazareth, whom ye crucified, whom God raised from the dead, even by him doth this man stand here before you whole. 11This is the stone which was set at nought of you builders, which is become the head of the corner. 12Neither is there salvation in any other: for there is none other name under heaven given among men, whereby we must be saved."

1 Peter 2:7–8 "7Unto you therefore which believe he is precious: but unto them which be disobedient, the stone which the builders disallowed, the same is made the head of the corner, 8And a stone of stumbling, and a rock of offence, even to them which stumble at the word, being disobedient: whereunto also they were appointed."

Romans 9:33, "As it is written, Behold, I lay in Sion a stumblingstone and rock of offence: and whosoever believeth on him shall not be ashamed."

Isaiah 28:16, "Therefore thus saith the Lord God, Behold, I lay in Zion for a foundation a stone, a tried stone, a precious corner stone, a sure foundation: he that believeth shall not make haste."

Now I can see that the Ark is a picture of a grace period: as long as the Ark was being built there was hope for everyone. Nowhere in the story of Noah did God say no one else could get in the Ark. God said he is building the Ark to save Noah and his household and some creatures, but God knew no one other than Noah's household would believe and act on God's word, but what the other people in the days of Noah did not know and let it pass them by was a grace period; when the Ark was finished and God closed the door of the Ark, the grace period was gone, and there were no more chances.

Looking at God in his character and his love for his creation, in reality, God did give the people that perished during the flood a chance between the time the Ark started being built till it was finished. That had anyone asked and believed what God had told Noah, they would have entered the Ark, but they were too blind and wicked.

The grace period we are in, just like Noah's days, has a beginning and ending; it started with Jesus being the first tree cut down to all the others that come afterward, and when the last pieces are put in the body, Christ will be just like the last pieces on the Ark and the door. God will close again, and the grace period we are in will be over, and just like in Noah's days, there will be a lot who will miss it and will be left behind to endure the destruction that comes after the body of Christ is completed, just like those in Noah's days.

John 3:16, "For God so loved the world, that he gave his only begotten Son, that whosoever believeth in him should not perish, but have everlasting life."

1 Thessalonians 5:3, "For when they shall say, Peace and safety; then sudden destruction cometh upon them, as travail upon a woman with child; and they shall not escape."

The building of the Ark is where we are at in the grace period we are living in as well as the believers alive in my days and other believers to come later during the building of the body of Christ.

I am waiting on the finished work of the body of Christ, where Noah is done, completed, and is in the history of the Word of God to be reread, examined, and studied.

Everything after the building of the Ark is a picture of things yet to come in our days, while in Noah's days, everything after the building of the Ark is a shadow and picture that run parallel to the days we are in.

This is very important to understand: the building of the Ark is the grace period, from Jesus's death to the Rapture or calling away, because destruction did not come till the Ark was done. And God-chosen people were safe from what was coming. It is going to be the same for us in Christ today: before and after that comes to the Lord and Savior all the way to the Rapture.

When I look at the building of the Ark, I can see my hope in the Lord, beyond the building of the Ark: the Rapture, seven years of tribulation, marriage supper, the two witnesses, and the New Jerusalem city coming down.

All these events can be seen after the building of the Ark, but again I know I am in the part of the story of Noah that is the building of the Ark, but as Paul Harvey would say, here is the rest of the story. I cannot wait for the rest of Noah's story to be past tense in my time and all the born-again believers.' But in the meanwhile the body of Christ is still at the part of the story of the building of the Ark. And we are waiting for the rest of the story.

Matthew 22:14, "For many are called, but few are chosen."

I get even more understanding, knowing that in my days God's Word is talking about the body of Christ, but in Noah's days it would have been the trees, not the people, that were going to perish.

Noah goes to the forest, where he finds the trees but picks through them to transform them into the piece he needs, for the place it will be used, but not all will be used. And there is only a certain amount and position that will be needed.

I can see some being used for framing, rafting, wall, and siding.

Going back to Noah being the head over the building of the Ark, God is the head over building the body of Christ.

Noah was going by God's words of instruction; God is going by his own words as well.

Matthew 20:23 "And he saith unto them, Ye shall drink indeed of my cup, and be baptized with the baptism that I am baptized with: but to sit on my right hand, and on my left, is not mine to give, but it shall be given to them for whom it is prepared of my Father."

This is how I came to understand that God and Noah are a parallel or picture of our times and Noah's days, so when I look at Noah, I see God putting the body of Christ together like Noah with the building of the Ark.

God knew that Noah and his household would be the ones saved, and God knows how many in the body of Christ there will be. It is sad to know that when the Ark is done, many will perish, as well as when the body of Christ is done.

Not just the Ark shows the body of Christ, but it was shown to me with the making of Eve.

Genesis 2:18, "And the Lord God said, it is not good that the man should be alone; I will make him an help meet for him."

For me to understand this, I needed to understand a helpmeet, which is a woman and a bride, also later a wife.

Genesis 2:21–25 "²¹And the Lord God caused a deep sleep to fall upon Adam, and he slept: and he took one of his ribs, and closed up the flesh instead thereof; ²²And the rib, which the Lord God had taken from man, made he a woman, and brought her unto the man. ²³And Adam said, this is now bone of my bones, and flesh of my flesh: she shall be called Woman, because she was taken out of Man. ²⁴Therefore shall a man leave his father and his mother, and shall cleave unto his wife: and they shall be one flesh. [25]And they were both naked, the man and his wife, and were not ashamed."

This event is a picture of the body of Christ, the bride of Christ, the Rapture, and the supper of the Lamb as well.

Now we bring in the event of Jesus being crucified.

John 19:30, "When Jesus therefore had received the vinegar, he said, It is finished: and he bowed his head, and gave up the ghost."

John 19:34, "But one of the soldiers with a spear pierced his side, and forthwith came there out blood and water."

There is a lot here; first I look at the comparison of Adam and Jesus.

Adam was put in a deep sleep, and so was Jesus. When I study sleep in the Word, it often uses this word as a symbol for death. One represents flesh, the other represents spirit.

Luke 8:52, "And all wept, and bewailed her: but he said, Weep not; she is not dead, but sleepeth."

Matthew 9:24, "He said unto them, Give place: for the maid is not dead, but sleepeth. And they laughed him to scorn."

Daniel 12:2, "And many of them that sleep in the dust of the earth shall awake, some to everlasting life, and some to shame and everlasting contempt."

Adam was put in a deep sleep, and so was Jesus. Adam had one rib removed from him, for God to create a woman, which is a picture of flesh.

Jesus had his rib removed while he was in a deep sleep; Jesus had already given up the ghost when he got pierced. The blood and water that came out was the spiritual rib.

This is to create the bride of Christ, and Adam's rib is to create his bride, Eve.

In the days of Noah and Adam, their events are done, but in the days, we are in we are still in the building of the Ark and the making of Eve.

The spiritual rib of Jesus is still being formed today. And when completed, it will be the bride of Christ, which is God-chosen, and as God took Eve to Adam, so will God take the Church to Jesus; this is also a picture of the Rapture and the Lamb's supper when God take Eve to Adam.

Here are two events that reveal the building of the of the body of Christ, which is the building of the Ark and the making of Eve. In both events, it is clear the Rapture takes place as soon as the building is done.

This is what convinced me that the Rapture will take place once the building is completed.

Both the building of the Ark and making of Eve from the rib of Adam are the picture of the grace period that we are in, and in both cases, God takes both Noah and his household to save them, and Eve to give to Adam.

2 Timothy 1:9, "Who hath saved us, and called us with an holy calling, not according to our works, but according to his own purpose and grace, which was given us in Christ Jesus before the world began."

Ephesians 2:8–9, [8]"For by grace are ye saved through faith; and that not of yourselves: it is the gift of God: [9]Not of works, lest any man should boast."

Romans 6:14, "For sin shall not have dominion over you: for ye are not under the law, but under grace."

Romans 11:6, "And if by grace, then is it no more of works: otherwise grace is no more grace. But if it be of works, then it is no more grace: otherwise work is no more work."

These scriptures got me to understand that God is doing the work, not me.

Philippians 1:6, "Being confident of this very thing, that he which hath begun a good work in you will perform it until the day of Jesus Christ."

When I look at Eve and consider what she had to do with any part of herself being created, I wonder whether she chose her blood type, eyes color, hair color, height, body build.

Eve had nothing to do with anything about her being created; God just created her with Adam's rib.

The same thing happens with Jesus's spiritual rib; it has been removed and now is under construction and is even being constructed while I draft this book and however long he got to finish the body of Christ, he will complete it. Nothing can stop him and his building the bride of Christ.

Matthew 16:18, "And I say also unto thee, that thou art Peter, and upon this rock I will build my church; and the gates of hell shall not prevail against it."

Noah building the Ark showed me the same thing that Eve showed me.

Noah is a picture of God, and his three sons are a picture of the Trinity. Now God is three in one, which are the Father, the Son, and the Holy Ghost. Yes, Noah and his sons are doing the work on the Ark, but what was revealed to me is that the Father gives his Son the Word that became flesh and paid the wages of my sins and the world's sins, and then the comforter comes after the Son ascends back to the Father. This is God showing how he is building the Church.

This is a picture how God in three is and has built my salvation and others' as well.

Romans 10:9, "That if thou shalt confess with thy mouth the Lord Jesus, and shalt believe in thine heart that God hath raised him from the dead, thou shalt be saved."

Ephesians 2:8, "For by grace are ye saved through faith; and that not of yourselves: it is the gift of God."

Titus 3:5, "Not by works of righteousness which we have done, but according to his mercy he saved us, by the washing of regeneration, and renewing of the Holy Ghost."

Acts 4:12, "Neither is there salvation in any other: for there is none other name under heaven given among men, whereby we must be saved."

John 3:17–18 "17For God sent not his Son into the world to condemn the world; but that the world through him might be saved. 18He that believeth on him is not condemned: but he that believeth not is condemned already, because he hath not believed in the name of the only begotten Son of God."

The story of Noah goes very deep in revealing the days that we are in; both the days of Noah and the present time that we live in concerning the salvation needed both for the days of Noah and a grace period from the death of Jesus Christ and the present time that I am in and all the way to when the Rapture takes place are considered a grace period.

The destruction in Noah's days and in the grace period of my time will not happen until the work of the building is done.

Looking again at the building of the Ark, Noah used gopher wood to build the Ark, and God is using born-again souls to build the Church, the bride of Christ, and New Jerusalem, which are the same, just like my mother: she is a mother, wife, sister, aunt, grandmother, and employee. Same person but different identities.

Noah also coated it with pitch inside and out as God instructed. This is a picture of God coating his born-again believers with the Holy Ghost, sometimes called comforter, which makes the body one in Christ Jesus, just like the pitch makes the Ark one.

John 16:7, "Nevertheless I tell you the truth; It is expedient for you that I go away: for if I go not away, the Comforter will not come unto you; but if I depart, I will send him unto you."

John 14:26, "But the Comforter, which is the Holy Ghost, whom the Father will send in my name, he shall teach you all things, and bring all things to your remembrance, whatsoever I have said unto you."

1 Corinthians 2:9–13 "9But as it is written, Eye hath not seen, nor ear heard, neither have entered into the heart of man, the things which God hath prepared for them that love him. 10But God hath revealed

them unto us by his Spirit: for the Spirit searcheth all things, yea, the deep things of God. [11]For what man knoweth the things of a man, save the spirit of man which is in him? even so the things of God knoweth no man, but the Spirit of God. [12]Now we have received, not the spirit of the world, but the spirit which is of God; that we might know the things that are freely given to us of God. [13]Which things also we speak, not in the words which man's wisdom teacheth, but which the Holy Ghost teacheth, comparing spiritual things with spiritual."

John 16:13 "Howbeit when he, the Spirit of truth, is come, he will guide you into all truth: for he shall not speak of himself; but whatsoever he shall hear, that shall he speak: and he will shew you things to come."

John 14:17, "Even the Spirit of truth; whom the world cannot receive, because it seeth him not, neither knoweth him: but ye know him; for he dwelleth with you, and shall be in you."

Matthew 10:20, "For it is not ye that speak, but the Spirit of your Father which speaketh in you."

Galatians 4:6, "And because ye are sons, God hath sent forth the Spirit of his Son into your hearts, crying, Abba, Father."

First God sent his word down from generation to generation to the children of Israel, to show and tell of his Son Jesus coming and of the events that will happen when he is here. Then his Son arrived and fulfilled the prophecies and the laws given in the Old Testament all the way up to his death.

The disobedience of one man against God happened at the beginning with Adam, and the wages of that disobedience is death.

The death of Jesus Christ, the Son of God, King of kings, Lord of lords, was given as a gift to humankind to pay every wages of disobedience, sin, and ungodliness in everything that has ever been done under the sun, past, present, and future, and was paid for in full of the death of Jesus at Calvary, and all that humankind must do is believe that. Then we will receive the Holy Ghost, and he will be with us as believers forever. So we have the forgiveness of sin that's been paid for, and all I had to do was accept it; believe in the son of God that he died for my sins and that alone saves me, but then the Holy Spirit came in me to teach me, correct me, and change the old man to a new way, so he uses the Word of God and his authority and his power within me to shape and mold me for the body of Christ and the position I will be in it, just like how Noah and his sons took the trees of gopher and shaped it to fit what part of the boat of the Ark that it would be on and then seal with the pitch to make it one solid Ark, just like the Holy Ghost so that I would become one with the body of Christ.

Salvation is very important because of the danger that was coming for Noah in his days, as well as the time we are living in, but the Lord showed me another event that dealt with salvation.

Moses and the Hebrew children experienced salvation in their days, as well as when Moses said, "Stand still and see the salvation of the Lord," but this was twofold; it literally was their salvation against Egyptian soldiers that were coming after them, but the waters departed, and they were able to escape the danger that they were in. also a picture of salvation from the wrath of God because of the sins of humankind. When moses lifted the rod that is a picture of Jesus Crist being lifted up at the cross from salvation for humankind to be able to be saved. There was no other escape then other than what God provided, and there is no other escape for Noah and his days except for what God provided for them. And the same is true today; there is no other escape of the dangers that are coming to humankind other than what God has provided for us, but as for Moses it was showing the same as Noah was showing: how it affects our days and only the Holy Spirit can reveal this. I was in awe when the Lord showed this to me, but when Moses said, stand still and see the salvation of the Lord, the Holy Ghost revealed to me the picture of salvation.

Exodus 14:13–31 "¹³And Moses said unto the people, Fear ye not, standstill, and see the salvation of the Lord, which he will shew to you today: for the Egyptians whom ye have seen today, ye shall see them again no more forever. ¹⁴The Lord shall fight for you, and ye shall hold your peace. ¹⁵And the Lord said unto Moses, Wherefore criest thou unto me? speak unto the children of Israel, that they go forward: ¹⁶But lift thou up thy rod, and stretch out thine hand over the sea, and divide it: and the children of Israel shall go on dry ground through the midst of the sea. [17]And I, behold, I will harden the hearts of the Egyptians, and they shall follow them: and I will get me honour upon Pharaoh, and upon all his host, upon his chariots, and upon his horsemen. [18]And the Egyptians shall know that I am the Lord, when I have gotten me honour upon Pharaoh, upon his chariots, and upon his horsemen. [19]And the angel of God, which went before the camp of Israel, removed and went behind them; and the pillar of the cloud went from before their face, and stood behind them: [20]And it came between the camp of the Egyptians and the camp of Israel; and it was a cloud and darkness to them, but it gave light by night to these: so that the one came not near the other all the night. [21]And Moses stretched out his hand over the sea; and the Lord caused the sea to go back by a strong east wind all that night, and made the sea dry land, and the waters were divided. [22]And the children of Israel went into the midst of the sea upon the dry ground: and the waters were a wall unto them on their right hand, and on their left. [23]And the Egyptians pursued, and went in after them to the midst of the sea, even all Pharaoh's horses, his chariots, and his horsemen. [24]And it came to pass, that in the morning watch the Lord looked unto the host of the Egyptians through the pillar of fire and of the cloud, and troubled the host of the Egyptians, [25]And took off their chariot wheels, that they drave them heavily: so that the Egyptians said, Let us flee from the face of Israel; for the Lord fighteth for them against the Egyptians. [26]And the Lord said unto Moses, Stretch out thine hand over the sea, that the waters may come again upon the Egyptians, upon their chariots, and upon their horsemen. [27]And Moses stretched forth his hand over the sea, and the sea returned to his strength when the morning appeared; and the Egyptians fled against it; and the Lord overthrew the Egyptians in the midst of the sea. [28]And the waters returned, and covered the chariots, and the horsemen, and all the host of Pharaoh that came into the sea after them; there remained not so much as one of them. [29]But the children of Israel walked upon dry land in the midst of the sea; and the waters were a wall unto them on their right hand, and on their left. [30]Thus the Lord saved Israel that day out of the hand of the Egyptians; and Israel saw the Egyptians dead upon the sea shore. [31]And Israel saw that great work which the Lord did upon the Egyptians: and the people feared the Lord, and believed the Lord, and his servant Moses."

In this story the Lord had me to look at some key words and chew on them.

The cane that Moses had stretched over the sea, the name of the sea, Red Sea, the dividing of the sea, and the eastern wind.

Red Sea is a picture of the Old Testament. The reason I say that is because even in the Old Testament it represented the blood of animals for the sins of Israel's people, the Hebrew children, so the Red Sea the Lord got me understand is the Old Testament, and when Moses lifted up his cane and straightened out his arms over the sea, it is a picture of Jesus Christ, Son of God, being lifted up on the cross of Calvary so that the eastern wind could come and part the Red Sea, which is a picture of the Holy Ghost coming, which divides the water, which is a picture of the Old and New Testament.

Moses said stand still and see the salvation of the Lord; they saw their salvation for that day, but as for me with the Holy Ghost dwelling in me I can see my salvation in that picture that God created in that real-life story for me to read thousands of years later. Only God can do that.

That story alone I can see the Old Testament, I can see the death and resurrection of Jesus, I can see the Holy Ghost coming afterward, I can see the New Testament coming, I can see the believers walking and living in faith, which is the Word of God, and I can see the Rapture as the believers get the Promised Land, just like the Hebrew children got to the other side as well, but also I can see the death of all God's children's enemies.

What is amazing to me is God use these two real-life events to speak to me and others that can see it too.

The world cannot see it, because they are not looking with the right spirit; he is the one that wrote it, and he is the only one that can reveal the mystery of the Word of God.

What both of these stories let me know is that this is true: if God is for you, who can be against you?

Romans 8:31, "What shall we then say to these things? If God be for us, who can be against us?"

Noah knew that God was with him because I do not see anywhere in the story that he was worried or afraid.

I do not see in this story of Noah that Satan or his followers tried to stop the building of the Ark. It could have been God had a hedge around them like Job.

Job 1:10, "Hast not thou made an hedge about him, and about his house, and about all that he hath on every side? thou hast blessed the work of his hands, and his substance is increased in the land."

1 Peter 5:8, "Be sober, be vigilant; because your adversary the devil, as a roaring lion, walketh about, seeking whom he may devour."

Job 1:7, "And the Lord said unto Satan, Whence comest thou? Then Satan answered the Lord, and said, From going to and fro in the earth, and from walking up and down in it."

This is why the Lord does not want believers or me to fear, because Satan or anything else cannot hurt or harm his people unless allowed by God.

2 Timothy 1:7, "For God hath not given us the spirit of fear; but of power, and of love, and of a sound mind."

Psalms 56:3, "What time I am afraid, I will trust in thee."

Isaiah 41:10, "Fear thou not; for I am with thee: be not dismayed; for I am thy God: I will strengthen thee; yea, I will help thee; yea, I will uphold thee with the right hand of my righteousness."

Noah and Moses were not afraid of the threat that was coming, because they knew God and knew they could trust God. And this is why I am not afraid of what is coming in the days I am living, because I know what God has done for me.

I can also see how God told both men of God what was about to happen and what they had to do to escape.

God has allowed me to have the mouth of God the bible, and within the pages of his mouth, he tells me what is coming and how to escape it.

Daniel and the lion dens, Shadrach, Meshach, Abednego and the fire pit, and little David and the giant, along with Noah and Moses just did not become fearless and courageous overnight. These men grew in knowledge, wisdom, and understanding over a period, as God revealed himself to them to the point, or rather, whether they live or die, they knew God had the final say and would not at any cost turn from trusting God even if it meant death.

This is having a relationship and learning of God and what he can do.

The days I am living in are no different: I am to trust God with the plan of salvation, just as Noah did in his days. Noah did not focus on the danger coming or when it would get there; he just worked on the Ark with his sons till it was completed.

God just wants to work on me, as he sees fit too. He needs me to pray, read, and study his Word so the Holy Ghost can do his job on me because the hardest part is done on my behalf by Jesus, Son of God, has paid the wages of my sins with his death and not mine only but to all who will believe in him.

2 Timothy 2:15, "Study to shew thyself approved unto God, a workman that needeth not to be ashamed, rightly dividing the word of truth."

1 Thessalonians 5:16–18, [16]"Rejoice evermore. [17]Pray without ceasing. [18]In everything give thanks: for this is the will of God in Christ Jesus concerning you."

Romans 12:2, "And be not conformed to this world: but be ye transformed by the renewing of your mind, that ye may prove what is that good, and acceptable, and perfect, will of God."

1 Timothy 2:3–4, [3]"For this is good and acceptable in the sight of God our Saviour; [4]Who will have all men to be saved, and to come unto the knowledge of the truth."

I can only imagine what was going on during the time of Noah's days, as they were building the Ark. According to the Scriptures, we know that they were doing things that we are doing today partying and drinking, giving in marriages, and a lot of weakness going on, basically the same thing that is going on in our time and the days that we are living, trying to cut God out of everything, because if God had not intervened, there would not had been pure human DNA. And Satan is doing it in my days as well, by making it look as if God were a fairy tale, because Satan knows that it is by faith through grace that I am and anyone else can be saved, and his desire is to make it where no one will believe there's a God and that he forgives sins of the worse sinner, but there will come a time when no one can work, just like a lot in solemn Sodom and Gomorrah.

There was no more work that could be done, except pull out Abraham's relatives and just like when Lot and his family were pulled out, then destruction comes.

John 9:4, "I must work the works of him that sent me, while it is day: the night cometh, when no man can work."

What I have learned from the Scriptures is that in every incident, God's people always escape the destruction coming.

The Ark itself is not just a picture of the body of Christ but a picture of Jesus himself. And the door on the Ark when God closes the door is saying a lot. The church is gone.

John 10:9–16 "⁹I am the door: by me if any man enter in, he shall be saved, and shall go in and out, and find pasture. ¹⁰The thief cometh not, but for to steal, and to kill, and to destroy: I am come that they might have life, and that they might have it more abundantly. ¹¹I am the good shepherd: the good shepherd giveth his life for the sheep. ¹²But he that is an hireling, and not the shepherd, whose own the sheep are not, seeth the wolf coming, and leaveth the sheep, and fleeth: and the wolf catcheth them, and scattereth the sheep. ¹³The hireling fleeth, because he is an hireling, and careth not for the sheep. ¹⁴I am the good shepherd, and know my sheep, and am known of mine. ¹⁵As the Father knoweth me, even so know I the Father: and I lay down my life for the sheep. ¹⁶And other sheep I have, which are not of this fold: them also I must bring, and they shall hear my voice; and there shall be one-fold, and one shepherd."

John 10:7, "Then said Jesus unto them again, Verily, verily, I say unto you, I am the door of the sheep."

John 14:6, "Jesus saith unto him, I am the way, the truth, and the life: no man cometh unto the Father, but by me."

Ephesians 2:18, "For through him we both have access by one Spirit unto the Father."

The creatures going into the Ark are a picture of the saved believers.

Mark 16:15–16, [15]"And he said unto them, go ye into all the world, and preach the gospel to every creature. [16]He that believeth and is baptized shall be saved; but he that believeth not shall be damned."

God is inside the Ark already and tells Noah and his family to come in the Ark, and God himself will shut the door, because no one will be able to open it and is safe from the destruction about to start. What I like about this, again, is that no destruction could start till Noah, his household, and the creatures were safe in the Ark and the door was closed. It will be the same for my days, whether in the ground or alive at the Rapture, the seven-year tribulation will not start till the Bride is gone.

Revelation 3:7–8 "[7]And to the angel of the church in Philadelphia write; These things saith he that is holy, he that is true, he that hath the key of David, he that openeth, and no man shutteth; and shutteth, and no man openeth; [8]I know thy works: behold, I have set before thee an open door, and no man can shut it: for thou hast a little strength, and hast kept my word, and hast not denied my name."

Isaiah 22:22, "And the key of the house of David will I lay upon his shoulder; so he shall open, and none shall shut; and he shall shut, and none shall open."

Just a reminder from the start of the Ark being built to God closing the door on the Ark is a picture of the grace period that we are living in.

When the grace period is over, it will be the same as the Church being raptured. That door will be closed.

Once this grace period is over and a new salvation begins for those in the tribulation, it will not be as easy.

To me it reminds me how it would have been easier to graduate than have to get my GED; it was harder to get the GED than to graduate. This is the same for those that miss the Rapture versus going through the tribulation.

CHAPTER 4

THE RISE OF THE ARK

1 Thessalonians 4:16–18

> [16]For the Lord himself shall descend from heaven with a shout, with the voice of the archangel, and with the trump of God: and the dead in Christ shall rise first: [17]Then we which are alive and remain shall be caught up together with them in the clouds, to meet the Lord in the air: and so shall we ever be with the Lord. [18]Wherefore comfort one another with these words.

John 14:3, "And if I go and prepare a place for you, I will come again, and receive you unto myself; that where I am, there ye may be also."

1 Corinthians 15:50–53

> [50]Now this I say, brethren, that flesh and blood cannot inherit the kingdom of God; neither doth corruption inherit incorruption. [51]Behold, I shew you a mystery; We shall not all sleep, but we shall all be changed, [52]In a moment, in the twinkling of an eye, at the last trump: for the trumpet shall sound, and the dead shall be raised incorruptible, and we shall be changed. [53]For this corruptible must put on incorruption, and this mortal must put on immortality.

When the door of the Ark closed, this was and is a picture of the Rapture. That is going to happen sometime in my future, whether I am in the ground or alive on the earth.

The water below and the water coming down from the sky, causing the ark to rise, is the shadow of the Rapture.

The water symbolizes the Holy Ghost and the Word of God that causes the Rapture to take place.

John 19:34, "But one of the soldiers with a spear pierced his side, and forthwith came there out blood and water."

Blood and water here are a picture of the Holy Ghost and the Word of God. I cannot have one without the other, just like what James said about faith and work. I cannot have one without the other.

James 2:17–18

> [17]Even so faith, if it hath not works, is dead, being alone. [18]Yea, a man may say, thou hast faith, and I have works shew me thy faith without thy works, and I will shew thee my faith by my works.

I have come to understand the Word of God without the Holy Ghost is only good for reading it, because the Holy Ghost wrote it using different types of men to write it. And only the Holy Ghost can reveal what he wants to the reader.

2 Timothy 3:16–17

> [16]All scripture is given by inspiration of God, and is profitable for doctrine, for reproof, for correction, for instruction in righteousness: [17]That the man of God may be perfect, thoroughly furnished unto all good works.

To be born-again I must be born of blood and water, which is also the Holy Ghost and Word of God; also when he said I was saved by grace through faith is also the Holy Ghost and Word of God.

John 3:5, "Jesus answered, Verily, verily, I say unto thee, except a man be born of water and of the Spirit, he cannot enter into the kingdom of God."

Ephesians 2:8, "For by grace are ye saved through faith; and that not of yourselves: it is the gift of God."

This is a good day for Noah and his household and the creatures on the Ark with them, they get to escape the destruction, but is a bad day for them outside the Ark because they are going to suffer and die.

The days we are in, we are waiting on what already happened in Noah's days, and just like Noah's days, it too is going to be a great and terrible day.

Joel 2:11, "And the Lord shall utter his voice before his army: for his camp is very great: for he is strong that executeth his word: for the day of the Lord is great and very terrible; and who can abide it?"

I have come to understand that when Rapture happens, so will the seven-year tribulation. The door of the Ark being shut is not just a picture of the Rapture but also the start of the seven-year tribulation.

Revelation 3:10, "Because thou hast kept the word of my patience, I also will keep thee from the hour of temptation, which shall come upon all the world, to try them that dwell upon the earth."

In everything that I have read, whether it be Noah's story and the story of Sodom and Gomorrah, God always gets his people out of harm's way, before the harm ever gets there. The only times that he puts his people in harm's way are those who are not trusting in him or to correct them.

I can see this and the story of Jonah, who is running from God. I also can see it in the story of the man that Paul had said toward the church to give his flesh over to the devil to save his soul; this is also a picture of the seven-year tribulation because there will be those that will be saved during the tribulation that missed the Rapture and basically their flesh is turned over to the devil, who will rule the earth during the seven-year tribulation to save their souls, which will be refusing the mark of the beast and whether they make it through the tribulation or they die or are killed during the tribulation, because they refused to take the mark of the beast, this will be their salvation; they will literally be taking on what God's Son did for them and missed it but will have to suffer like God's Son Jesus and suffer as he did during the tribulation, because they will not be able to buy, sell, trade, or do anything basically living off the land, surviving the best they can, some being killed, tortured, starving, and naked, and so much terror, but yet by refusing the mark and selecting the consequences they will be saved.

2 Timothy 3:1–5

> ¹This know also, that in the last days perilous times shall come. ²For men shall be lovers of their own selves, covetous, boasters, proud, blasphemers, disobedient to parents, unthankful, unholy, ³Without natural affection, trucebreakers, false accusers, incontinent, fierce, despisers of those that are good, ⁴Traitors, heady, highminded, lovers of pleasures more than lovers of God; ⁵Having a form of godliness, but denying the power thereof: from such turn away.

Matthew 24:21, "For then shall be great tribulation, such as was not since the beginning of the world to this time, no, nor ever shall be."

The Rapture and the seven-year tribulation go hand in hand. When one happens the other starts.

The only difference in Noah's days is him and his household and the creatures in the Ark were the rapture from the destruction, which destroyed every living thing on dry land on earth. No one outside the Ark that lived on dry land survived.

The Rapture I and others in these days are waiting on will have those that are left behind.

Matthew 24:38–42

> ³⁸For as in the days that were before the flood they were eating and drinking, marrying and giving in marriage, until the day that No'e entered into the ark, ³⁹And knew not until the flood came, and took them all away; so shall also the coming of the Son of man be. ⁴⁰Then shall two be in the field; the one shall be taken, and the other left. ⁴¹Two women shall be grinding at the mill; the one shall be taken,

and the other left. [42]Watch therefore: for ye know not what hour your Lord doth come.

Luke 17:32–36

[32]Remember Lot's wife. [33]Whosoever shall seek to save his life shall lose it; and whosoever shall lose his life shall preserve it. [34]I tell you, in that night there shall be two men in one bed; the one shall be taken, and the other shall be left. [35]Two women shall be grinding together; the one shall be taken, and the other left. [36]Two men shall be in the field; the one shall be taken, and the other left.

Matthew 25:1–13

[1]Then shall the kingdom of heaven be likened unto ten virgins, which took their lamps, and went forth to meet the bridegroom. [2]And five of them were wise, and five were foolish. [3]They that were foolish took their lamps, and took no oil with them: [4]But the wise took oil in their vessels with their lamps. [5]While the bridegroom tarried, they all slumbered and slept. [6]And at midnight there was a cry made, Behold, the bridegroom cometh; go ye out to meet him. [7]Then all those virgins arose, and trimmed their lamps. [8]And the foolish said unto the wise, Give us of your oil; for our lamps are gone out. [9]But the wise answered, saying, Not so; lest there be not enough for us and you: but go ye rather to them that sell, and buy for yourselves. [10]And while they went to buy, the bridegroom came; and they that were ready went in with him to the marriage: and the door was shut. [11]Afterward came also the other virgins, saying, Lord, Lord, open to us. [12]But he answered and said, Verily I say unto you, I know you not. [13]Watch therefore, for ye know neither the day nor the hour wherein the Son of man cometh.

Those that are left behind will go through the worst times in the history of humankind. All because they love their life more and would not die to Christ Jesus, or they love pleasure more than God.

2 Timothy 3:1–9

> [1]This know also, that in the last days perilous times shall come. [2]For men shall be lovers of their own selves, covetous, boasters, proud, blasphemers, disobedient to parents, unthankful, unholy, [3]Without natural affection, trucebreakers, false accusers, incontinent, fierce, despisers of those that are good, [4]Traitors, heady, highminded, lovers of pleasures more than lovers of God; [5]Having a form of godliness, but denying the power thereof: from such turn away. [6]For of this sort are they which creep into houses, and lead captive silly women laden with sins, led away with divers lusts, [7]Ever learning, and never able to come to the knowledge of the truth. [8]Now as Jannes and Jambres withstood Moses, so do these also resist the truth: men of corrupt minds, reprobate concerning the faith. [9]But they shall proceed no further: for their folly shall be manifest unto all men, as their's also was.

This is why others, and I die to self and live in Christ Jesus. Yes, I am a sinner whose sin is paid for.

Noah and his household were saved by building and getting into the Ark.

Others and I in the grace period that we are living in are saved by grace through faith.

There are two things that I am convinced of; one is it appointed once for man to die then judgement, and the second is the Rapture will happen just as much as I am convinced the flood happened as well.

Hebrews 9:27, "And as it is appointed unto men once to die, but after this the judgment."

Isaiah 57:1–2

> [1]The righteous perisheth, and no man layeth it to heart: and merciful men are taken away, none considering that the righteous is taken away from the evil to come. [2]He shall

enter into peace: they shall rest in their beds, each one walking in his uprightness.

1 Thessalonians 4:16–17

> [16]For the Lord himself shall descend from heaven with a shout, with the voice of the archangel, and with the trump of God: and the dead in Christ shall rise first: [17]Then we which are alive and remain shall be caught up together with them in the clouds, to meet the Lord in the air: and so shall we ever be with the Lord.

I know there are only two places that I have a choice to go if I die before the Rapture. That is heaven or hell, so I have learned to be ready for the grave and heaven, but knowing if I am ready for the grave every day, I am sure to be ready for the Rapture as well.

Like what Hebrews 9:27 said about after death is judgment. And Luke 16:19–31 confirms this, by showing the only two destinations after death.

Luke 16:19–31

> [19]There was a certain rich man, which was clothed in purple and fine linen, and fared sumptuously every day: [20]And there was a certain beggar named Lazarus, which was laid at his gate, full of sores, [21]And desiring to be fed with the crumbs which fell from the rich man's table: moreover the dogs came and licked his sores. [22]And it came to pass, that the beggar died, and was carried by the angels into Abraham's bosom: the rich man also died, and was buried; [23]And in hell he lifts up his eyes, being in torments, and seeth Abraham afar off, and Lazarus in his bosom. [24]And he cried and said, Father Abraham, have mercy on me, and send Lazarus, that he may dip the tip of his finger in water, and cool my tongue; for I am tormented in this flame. [25]But Abraham said, Son, remember that thou in thy lifetime receivedst thy good things, and likewise Lazarus evil things: but now he is comforted, and thou art tormented. [26]And beside all this, between us and you there is a great gulf fixed: so that they

which would pass from hence to you cannot; neither can they pass to us, that would come from thence. [27]Then he said, I pray thee therefore, father, that thou wouldest send him to my father's house: [28]For I have five brethren; that he may testify unto them, lest they also come into this place of torment. [29]Abraham saith unto him, they have Moses and the prophets; let them hear them. [30]And he said, Nay, Father Abraham: but if one went unto them from the dead, they would repent. [31]And he said unto him, if they hear not Moses and the prophets, neither will they be persuaded, though one rose from the dead.

Rich man trusted in his richest not God, he also did not love his neighbor to help in his needs that the rich man could meet. Notting wrong being wealthy it help to give to others if they are in need. But the key to avoid the destination the rich man went is love God and your neighbor.

God is clear on the two great commandments.

Matthew 22:34–40

[34]But when the Pharisees had heard that he had put the Sadducees to silence, they were gathered together. [35]Then one of them, which was a lawyer, asked him a question, tempting him, and saying, [36]Master, which is the great commandment in the law? [37]Jesus said unto him, Thou shalt love the Lord thy God with all thy heart, and with all thy soul, and with all thy mind. [38]This is the first and great commandment. [39]And the second is like unto it, thou shalt love thy neighbour as thyself. [40]On these two commandments hang all the law and the prophets.

This really does not save me either, because I have to receive the greatest gift to humankind to be able to do the two great commandments.

Romans 6:23, "For the wages of sin is death; but the gift of God is eternal life through Jesus Christ our Lord."

John 3:16, "For God so loved the world, that he gave his only begotten Son, that whosoever believeth in him should not perish, but have everlasting life."

Romans 10:9–10

> [9]That if thou shalt confess with thy mouth the Lord Jesus, and shalt believe in thine heart that God hath raised him from the dead, thou shalt be saved. [10]For with the heart man believeth unto righteousness; and with the mouth confession is made unto salvation.

Acts 16:30–33

> [30]And brought them out, and said, Sirs, what must I do to be saved? [31]And they said, believe on the Lord Jesus Christ, and thou shalt be saved, and thy house. [32]And they spake unto him the word of the Lord, and to all that were in his house. [33]And he took them the same hour of the night, and washed their stripes; and was baptized, he and all his, straightway.

I learned not about what I can do, but what God has already done.

Humankind owed a debt that we could not pay for the wages of sin that was owed. That is why I read the story of the rich man and Lazarus. There are two holding spots with a gulf in between them, and neither one can cross to the other. It is because animal blood was not good enough to pay the wages of sins humankind owed so God could keep the old covenant and the children of God, who did trust and obey God, could stay at until God's Son would pay the wages for the entire world, all humankind, past, present, and future.

The moment Christ Jesus died, the dead in that holding spot were now able to be with Jesus when he ascended to God. And this was witnessed by many.

Matthew 27:51–53

> [51]And, behold, the veil of the temple was rent in twain from the top to the bottom; and the earth did quake, and the rocks rent; [52]And the graves were opened; and many

bodies of the saints which slept arose, [53]And came out of the graves after his resurrection, and went into the holy city, and appeared unto many.

Noah knew what he had to do to be saved from the destruction coming. And he did what needed to be done to make sure he and his household would be saved.

The importance of being ready for death or the Rapture is the fact that there is no in between. I and anyone else will be either in Jesus Christ or out of Jesus Christ to be saved from hell, just like being in the Ark or outside the Ark when the flood starts.

The beginning of the flood is the beginning of the end for those outside the Ark. And Rapture, when it happens, is the beginning of the end for a lot of those who miss it. It has not happened, so there is time for anyone to get ready.

Noah and his days are done as for their rapture or salvation, but all humankind that is breathing right now can continue getting ready, start getting ready, and return to getting ready.

How can I be ready? To start, believing that Jesus, Son of God, died for the wages of sins for me and the whole world.

John 3:16, "For God so loved the world, that he gave his only begotten Son, that whosoever believeth in him should not perish, but have everlasting life."

What does that mean? That my sins, past, present, and future, have been paid for, so I owe no more debt for my sins.

John 1:29, "The next day John seeth Jesus coming unto him, and saith, Behold the Lamb of God, which taketh away the sin of the world."

How do I know he did pay for my sins? By faith.

Romans 1:17, "For therein is the righteousness of God revealed from faith to faith: as it is written, the just shall live by faith."

What is faith? The Word of God.

Romans 10:17, "So then faith cometh by hearing, and hearing by the word of God."

Jesus died for me and the world knowing the sinful state the world and I were in, but died anyway, but not everyone is as sinful as some are. Some are worse than others, but my goodness or righteousness will not save me.

Isaiah 64:6, "But we are all as an unclean thing, and all our righteousnesses are as filthy rags; and we all do fade as a leaf; and our iniquities, like the wind, have taken us away."

Ephesians 2:8–10

> [8]For by grace are ye saved through faith; and that not of yourselves: it is the gift of God: [9]Not of works, lest any man should boast. [10]For we are his workmanship, created in Christ Jesus unto good works, which God hath before ordained that we should walk in them.

I got to believe by faith that Jesus paid for my sins and will work on me as to what needs to be done.

Just as Noah and his household were safe in the Ark, I am safe in Jesus. This is what the Ark is: a picture of being in Jesus. This is why a child of God will be raptured, because as the Ark started to raise from the flood of Noah's days and everyone in that Ark were safe, everyone is safe in Jesus as well.

I do realize that knowing that my sins are paid for in full does not give me a license to sin or even pick and choose the sins I can do, but at the same time I cannot let my failure or sins keep me from having faith; my sins are paid for regardless of me. The following scriptures help me understand this.

Romans 6:1–2, "[1]What shall we say then? Shall we continue in sin, that grace may abound? [2]God forbid. How shall we, that are dead to sin, live any longer therein?"

Luke 18:9–14

> 9And he spake this parable unto certain which trusted in themselves that they were righteous, and despised others: 10Two men went up into the temple to pray; the one a Pharisee, and the other a publican. 11The Pharisee stood and prayed thus with himself, God, I thank thee, that I am not as other men are, extortioners, unjust, adulterers, or even as this publican. 12I fast twice in the week, I give tithes of all that I possess. 13And the publican, standing afar off, would not lift up so much as his eyes unto heaven, but smote upon his breast, saying, God be merciful to me a sinner. 14I tell you, this man went down to his house justified rather than the other: for everyone that exalteth himself shall be abased; and he that humbleth himself shall be exalted.

I learned a few things about these scriptures. One is that this is the reason many will miss the Rapture.

The pharisee is boasting to himself about how righteous he is and the righteous works he does. The sad thing about it is what he has done, not what God has done. No matter how righteous I am, it is still not good enough for my wages of sins or anyone else 's righteousness for their wages of sins. It must be the righteousness of Jesus Christ, not oneself, and by faith believing my sins are paid for, without doubting it. This is for anyone, not just me.

This is what Jesus was talking about with Pharisees in Luke 7:35–50

> 35But wisdom is justified of all her children. 36And one of the Pharisees desired him that he would eat with him. And he went into the Pharisee's house, and sat down to meat. 37And, behold, a woman in the city, which was a sinner, when she knew that Jesus sat at meat in the Pharisee's house, brought an alabaster box of ointment, 38And stood at his feet behind him weeping, and began to wash his feet with tears, and did wipe them with the hairs of her head, and kissed his feet, and anointed them with the ointment. 39Now when the Pharisee which had bidden him saw it, he

spake within himself, saying, this man, if he were a prophet, would have known who and what manner of woman this is that toucheth him: for she is a sinner. [40]And Jesus answering said unto him, Simon, I have somewhat to say unto thee. And he saith, Master, say on. [41]There was a certain creditor which had two debtors: the one owed five hundred pence, and the other fifty. [42]And when they had nothing to pay, he frankly forgave them both. Tell me therefore, which of them will love him most? [43]Simon answered and said, I suppose that he, to whom he forgave most. And he said unto him, thou hast rightly judged. [44]And he turned to the woman, and said unto Simon, Seest thou this woman? I entered into thine house, thou gavest me no water for my feet: but she hath washed my feet with tears, and wiped them with the hairs of her head. [45]Thou gavest me no kiss: but this woman since the time I came in hath not ceased to kiss my feet. [46]My head with oil thou didst not anoint but this woman hath anointed my feet with ointment. [47]Wherefore I say unto thee, her sins, which are many, are forgiven; for she loved much: but to whom little is forgiven, the same loveth little. [48]And he said unto her, thy sins are forgiven. [49]And they that sat at meat with him began to say within themselves, who is this that forgives sins also? [50]And he said to the woman, thy faith hath saved thee; go in peace.

The publican and the woman knew who they were, sinners and not just sinners, but sinners that needed help to change. They both knew who God and Jesus are and knew what they could do to help them.

I can be the top sinner, and everyone else could have but just one or two faults or sins within their life or heart, but regardless of one being greater or smaller in sin or even greater than me in righteousness, every one of us got to confess our sins and believe Jesus died and paid for our sins without doubting, and he would do the rest that is needed.

1 Timothy 1:15, "This is a faithful saying, and worthy of all acceptations, that Christ Jesus came into the world to save sinners; of whom I am chief."

1 John 1:9, "If we confess our sins, he is faithful and just to forgive us our sins, and to cleanse us from all unrighteousness."

John 4:24, "God is a Spirit: and they that worship him must worship him in spirit and in truth."

I have learned that God just wants me to be honest and true with him; after all, I cannot hide anything from him anyway, just like the publican, no matter how bad it is.

John's letters to the seven churches show this when he tells them all their good but then tells them what was wrong that they needed to correct and tells them the consequences if they do not correct what the Lord has pointed out to them to correct. This is God working on them and me as part of the Church; this is how he works on me as well and anyone else that's part of the body of the Church.

Revelation 2:3–5

> ³And hast borne, and hast patience, and for my name's sake hast labored, and hast not fainted. ⁴Nevertheless I have somewhat against thee, because thou hast left thy first love. ⁵Remember therefore from whence thou art fallen, and repent, and do the first works; or else I will come unto thee quickly, and will remove thy candlestick out of his place, except thou repent.

I cannot continue and sin just because I know my sins are paid for in full, but knowing that my sins are paid for and that my God is faithful and true to forgive me when he reveals whatever he is dealing with me on or to change, because he has begun the good work and he is faithful and true to finish it and just like Jonah and the whale he's able to do that work, get me to understand, and see what it is that he's dealing with me on. Even Paul the chief of sinners: he claimed and asked God to take out the thorns in his side three times, and God said that his grace is sufficient for him, so no matter how less I feel or how great I feel in the Kingdom of God, it is his grace that is accomplishing what needs to be done in me. This is because we are saved by grace through faith. The grace is the Holy Ghost, and the faith is the Word of God. In other words, the Word to God tells me what needs to be done or corrected, and the Holy Ghost empowers me to do it.

John 14:26, "But the Comforter, which is the Holy Ghost, whom the Father will send in my name, he shall teach you all things, and bring all things to your remembrance, whatsoever I have said unto you."

Philippians 4:13, "I can do all things through Christ which strengtheneth me."

The Rapture is getting closer. Every day that goes by, the Rapture or the grave is coming closer, just the same as Noah and his sons' work on the Ark. The closer the building was getting done, the closer to the flood they were getting as well. And the door of the Ark will be closed and is closed.

The Rapture that others and I are waiting for will be here. It has not yet come. And the grave will be here too if the Rapture has not come yet when my time is up. Either way I got to be ready for the grave first; that way if I am called up while waiting on the grave, it means I was ready for the Rapture.

John 10:7–9

> [7]Then said Jesus unto them again, Verily, verily, I say unto you, I am the door of the sheep. [8]All that ever came before me are thieves and robbers: but the sheep did not hear them. [9]I am the door: by me if any man enter in, he shall be saved, and shall go in and out, and find pasture.

The door of the Ark is a picture of Jesus as well as Noah, and everything and everyone with him was saved because they went through that door when God told them to come in. Just as that door closed, they were saved, and so is everyone that calls on Jesus and abides in him; if not, those will be left for the seven-year tribulation. The door of the Ark was Noah and his family salvation like Jesus is the door to humankind salvation after Jesus Christ sacrifice.

The raising of the Ark and the waters coming down and up is the picture of the Rapture and the seven-year tribulation, like I said earlier; it happens at the same time.

John 15:1–10

¹I am the true vine, and my Father is the husbandman. ²Every branch in me that beareth not fruit he taketh away: and every branch that beareth fruit, he purgeth it, that it may bring forth more fruit. ³Now ye are clean through the word which I have spoken unto you. ⁴Abide in me, and I in you. As the branch cannot bear fruit of itself, except it abide in the vine; no more can ye, except ye abide in me. ⁵I am the vine, ye are the branches: He that abideth in me, and I in him, the same bringeth forth much fruit: for without me ye can do nothing. ⁶If a man abide not in me, he is cast forth as a branch, and is withered; and men gather them, and cast them into the fire, and they are burned. ⁷If ye abide in me, and my words abide in you, ye shall ask what ye will, and it shall be done unto you. ⁸Herein is my Father glorified, that ye bear much fruit; so shall ye be my disciples. ⁹As the Father hath loved me, so have I loved you: continue ye in my love. ¹⁰If ye keep my commandments, ye shall abide in my love; even as I have kept my Father's commandments, and abide in his love. This goes back to the work God is doing on me and others. I must be in Jesus so that God, the husbandman, can work on me because I am the branch that he wants to bear fruits on, as well as others, as in Galatians 5:22–23, "²²But the fruit of the Spirit is love, joy, peace, longsuffering, gentleness, goodness, faith, ²³Meekness, temperance: against such there is no law."

This is what others, and I are being worked on to change from flesh fruits like hate, jealousy, greed.

2 Peter 3:9, "The Lord is not slack concerning his promise, as some men count slackness; but is longsuffering to us-ward, not willing that any should perish, but that all should come to repentance."

God is the top government; there is nothing over him, with no authority that is greater than his authority or to which he is accountable.

Hebrews 6:13, "For when God made promise to Abraham, because he could swear by no greater, he sware by himself."

Genesis 22:16, "And said, by myself have I sworn, saith the LORD, for because thou hast done this thing, and hast not withheld thy son, thine only son."

I have understood that God is above all, and all is under God, but when God must make an executive decision, such as the flood, Sodom and Gomorrah, and the Tower of Babel, something has gotten out of hand. Then God acts, keeping in mind that he knows the beginning to the end of days and every action in between. There is nothing that can out smart or out do him. And when he does act, there is no telling how patient God was until he decided to act.

Psalms 139:2–3, [2]"Thou knowest my downsitting and mine uprising, thou understandest my thought afar off. [3]Thou compassest my path and my lying down, and art acquainted with all my ways."

Hebrews 4:13, "Neither is there any creature that is not manifest in his sight: but all things are naked and opened unto the eyes of him with whom we have to do."

Matthew 10:30, "But the very hairs of your head are all numbered."

When the Rapture does happen it will be right on time, like it was in Noah's days with the flood, but then at the same time the seven years of tribulation start, just like the days of Noah when the door closed and then the floods came.

The seven-year tribulation will start after the Rapture, and it will be the worst event in the history of humankind, but this too, shows the love God has for humankind that he created, to try to get them to turn from their wicked ways.

Revelation 3:10, "Because thou hast kept the word of my patience, I also will keep thee from the hour of temptation, which shall come upon all the world, to try them that dwell upon the earth."

The Church will miss the tribulation because we will be called up, but the last days started when Jesus died on the cross, just like when Noah started building the Ark. The door was closed, and people and creatures died, but the difference in the grace period we are in is that after the Rapture those that are left behind will wish to die, rather than repent.

2 Timothy 3:1–5

> [1]This know also, that in the last days perilous times shall come. [2]For men shall be lovers of their own selves, covetous, boasters, proud, blasphemers, disobedient to parents, unthankful, unholy, [3]Without natural affection, trucebreakers, false accusers, incontinent, fierce, despisers of those that are good, [4]Traitors, heady, highminded, lovers of pleasures more than lovers of God; [5]Having a form of godliness, but denying the power thereof: from such turn away.

Matthew 24:21, "For then shall be great tribulation, such as was not since the beginning of the world to this time, no, nor ever shall be."

The more I live by faith, the more faith becomes reality. And I can clearly see in the Holy Ghost what he is revealing to me from the Word of God. The more I see, the more I cannot unsee, but it does enrich me in wisdom, knowledge, and understanding that I cannot attain in any other way, but by the Holy Ghost, through the Word of God, because the Holy Ghost will reveal what he wants me to see, for example, when he showed me this thought about being able to see or being blind.

Genesis 19:11, "And they smote the men that were at the door of the house with blindness, both small and great: so that they wearied themselves to find the door."

Genesis 21:18–19

> [18]Arise, lift up the lad, and hold him in thine hand; for I will make him a great nation. [19]And God opened her eyes, and she saw a well of water; and she went, and filled the bottle with water, and gave the lad drink.

Genesis 22:13 And Abraham lifted up his eyes, and looked, and behold behind him a ram caught in a thicket by his horns: and Abraham went and took the ram, and offered him up for a burnt offering in the stead of his son.

2 Corinthians 4:3, "But if our gospel be hid, it is hid to them that are lost."

Matthew 11:25, "At that time Jesus answered and said, I thank thee, O Father, Lord of heaven and earth, because thou hast hid these things from the wise and prudent, and hast revealed them unto babes."

The Lord got me to understand that he can open my eyes or blind them. That is why he said, "You have not because you do not ask, and when you ask you ask amiss."

James 4:2–3 ²Ye lust, and have not: ye kill, and desire to have, and cannot obtain: ye fight and war, yet ye have not, because ye ask not. ³Ye ask, and receive not, because ye ask amiss, that ye may consume it upon your lusts.

King Solomon shows what to ask for, understanding to judge rightly for his calling instead of silver or gold.

1 Kings 3:9–13

> ⁹Give therefore thy servant an understanding heart to judge thy people, that I may discern between good and bad: for who is able to judge this thy so great a people? ¹⁰And the speech pleased the LORD, that Solomon had asked this thing. ¹¹And God said unto him, Because thou hast asked this thing, and hast not asked for thyself long life; neither hast asked riches for thyself, nor hast asked the life of thine enemies; but hast asked for thyself understanding to discern judgment; ¹²Behold, I have done according to thy words: lo, I have given thee a wise and an understanding heart; so that there was none like thee before thee, neither after thee shall any arise like unto thee. ¹³And I have also given thee that which thou hast not asked, both riches, and honour: so that there shall not be any among the kings like unto thee all thy days.

This is what makes me understand what the Lord said, seek the kingdom and everything else will be added.

Matthew 6:33, "But seek ye first the kingdom of God, and his righteousness; and all these things shall be added unto you."

I learned to ask for wisdom, knowledge, and understanding from the Lord, instead of asking for silver or gold, which comes from the Word of God and the Holy Ghost, and bring forth what allows to come from the seeking as for revenue or rewards, just like Solomon after he asked God, and then God told him not only was he going to give him what he asked for but also what he did not ask for.

The Lord got me to stop trying to search the Scriptures with my on understanding, but with him and let him open my eyes to his Word and reveal what he chooses to reveal to me.

It is important being able to know what Abraham said to the rich man while he comforted Lazarus, after he asked for him to send someone from the grave.

Luke 16:27–31

> [27]Then he said, I pray thee therefore, father, that thou wouldest send him to my father's house: [28]For I have five brethren; that he may testify unto them, lest they also come into this place of torment. [29]Abraham saith unto him, They have Moses and the prophets; let them hear them. [30]And he said, Nay, Father Abraham: but if one went unto them from the dead, they will repent. [31]And he said unto him, If they hear not Moses and the prophets, neither will they be persuaded, though one rose from the dead.

This rich man wanted to warn his brothers of this horrible place, but he knew it would take something like someone coming from the grave.

Abraham reminded him that they had Moses and the prophets; if they did not hear from them, they would not be persuaded if one rose from the dead.

Jesus had not died yet, because Abraham was still across from the rich man, and after the death and resurrection of Jesus, this side of Abraham would be empty.

They were still under the old covenant, so they had Moses and the prophets and even could have the writing of some of the early books of the Old Testament. Abraham said that was enough for those still alive in their flesh.

These days that others and I are living in right now, we have Moses and the prophets as well, and not just that, we have one that rose from the grave, and his name is Jesus. And this is why we the family of God will be able to be risen from the grave and in a twinkling of an eye be transformed in the Rapture.

The Bible, Old and New Testament, wages of sins paid for, the Holy Ghost dwelling in born-again believers, and being able to know and see what prophets have longed to see.

Matthew 13:17, "For verily I say unto you, that many prophets and righteous men have desired to see those things which ye see, and have not seen them; and to hear those things which ye hear, and have not heard them."

I am able every day to see what the prophets of old desired to see, when I pick up my Bible and bring to life the events from Genesis to Revelation, as I read each book. And yet it plays in my mind and soul as I read it each time. With the help of the one that has seen it all, and had it written for all to have the Word of God, the Holy Ghost.

All of this being said, it makes sense why Jesus would say to his generation in Luke 11:31–32:

> [31]The queen of the south shall rise up in the judgment with the men of this generation, and condemn them: for she came from the utmost parts of the earth to hear the wisdom of Solomon; and, behold, a greater than Solomon is here. [32]The men of Nineve shall rise up in the judgment with this generation, and shall condemn it: for they repented at the preaching of Jonas; and, behold, a greater than Jonas is here.

I can only imagine my generation, what we have and know. What we have been blessed with, what they would say about each generation from the death of Jesus to my generation, and then to the Rapture.

I keep in mind what was said in Revelation 14:13, "And I heard a voice from heaven saying unto me, Write, Blessed are the dead which die in the Lord from henceforth: Yea, saith the Spirit, that they may rest from their labours; and their works do follow them."

This makes me think of everyone in the grace period, from the death of Jesus up to the Rapture, are blessed and their work follow; also when they leave their body, each one will know their doom, just like the rich man and Lazarus. The only thing one is waiting on after death is either their final sentence or waiting on the inheritance of God.

Death is final, there is no do-over. There is no "if I'm wrong, I wait on God to tell me when I get there." This is the cold hard truth; if I do not get it right on this side of heaven, as the rich man testified in the scripture, there was nothing he could do to change his situation or get word back to his brothers, and God did not tell him when he got there but let his destination and situation tell him.

The door of the Ark closed is a picture of the Rapture coming for all in the grave and those not in the grave, but also the start of the seven-year tribulation.

I come to understand that what God is expecting when He comes back is me to have faith and be busy about his business, day by day, trusting and obeying, knowing that no one knows when he is coming to gather up in his Church.

I myself have been on the focus of the Rapture of how close we are to it. When the Holy Ghost revealed all this to me, he got me to understand clearly were I am in the story of the days of Noah and what is going to happen, as well as the order in which it will happen. Not that I am smart, intelligent, or a genius, but the Holy Ghost just chose to let me see and understand and not hide it from me.

John 15:15, "Henceforth I call you not servants; for the servant knoweth not what his lord doeth: but I have called you friends; for all things that I have heard of my Father I have made known unto you."

This is why God told Abraham what he was going to do with Solomon and Gomorrah. God literally revealed his word and what his words were going to do because while Abraham was sitting there talking to God, he was hearing God's words that would be written down for us to read over and over and over again, but it does not change that this is God's word, and his word was revealed to him in real time.

Isaiah 41:8, "But thou, Israel, art my servant, Jacob whom I have chosen, the seed of Abraham my friend."

This is the picture of that; God showing me with the life event with Abraham and his conversation, as he was going to and judge Sodom and Gomorrah.

Regardless of what was going on around me or what God revealed to me, I keep my relationship with God and discuss with him if maybe I can change God's mind on the matter to be.

I learn just like Adam, Eve, and Abraham that when God shows up that is the time to fellowship with him because when I feel his presence, he wants to fellowship and discuss with me and me with him.

Lot and his family were rushed to get out of town by the two angels because they could not do anything until they were out of town. This is another thing that was revealed to me. The why Lot and his family escaped the judgment of the town is just the same as when the church misses the destruction coming in the seven-year tribulation, by being carried away in the Rapture.

Luke 18:8, "I tell you that he will avenge them speedily. Nevertheless when the Son of man cometh, shall he find faith on the earth?"

This is the key, having faith, which is the Word of God, that the world with the anti-spirit is trying to get altogether erased from earth so no one will have it; after all, that is where faith comes from and why it is continually attacked. And faith is how I know the story of Noah, the

Rapture, the seven-year tribulation, and so much more. Without it, I know nothing.

Romans 10:17, "So then faith cometh by hearing, and hearing by the word of God."

CHAPTER 5

THE FLOATING OF THE ARK

The Ark in my mind is floating along the top of the waters after the water above and the water below stop flowing out. The sun is out with nothing to do but wait on the water to descend, which will take about 150 days before Noah could get out.

This made me think of Isaiah 40:31, "But they that wait upon the Lord shall renew their strength; they shall mount up with wings as eagles; they shall run, and not be weary; and they shall walk, and not faint" and Psalms 27:14, "Wait on the Lord: be of good courage, and he shall strengthen thine heart: wait, I say, on the Lord." Also Psalm 37:7–9:

> [7]Rest in the Lord, and wait patiently for him: fret not thyself because of him who prospered in his way, because of the man who bringeth wicked devices to pass. [8]Cease from anger, and forsake wrath: fret not thyself in any wise to do evil. [9]For evildoers shall be cut off: but those that wait upon the Lord, they shall inherit the earth.

This scripture as well: Psalm 130:5, "I wait for the Lord, my soul doth wait, and in his word do, I hope." And finally, Habakkuk 2:3, "For the vision is yet for an appointed time, but at the end it shall speak, and not lie: though it tarries, wait for it; because it will surely come, it will not tarry."

Noah is waiting on the Lord till the water descends to be able to get out of the Ark, but meanwhile they are in the Ark waiting to do whatever they would be doing in the Ark.

Noah, even after the door closed on the Ark, waited on the Lord seven days before the flood started.

This grace period in the days I am living in is waiting on the Rapture, the supper in heaven, the tribulation, Armageddon, the millennium, and the destruction of Satan for once and all, and then eternity.

The picture of the Ark floating is a picture of supper time in heaven and the marriage of the Lamb while the tribulation is still going on under the Ark.

God closing the door of the Ark is a picture of the Rapture. And the floating of the Ark is a picture of the marriage of the Lamb and the supper.

Others and I are still waiting on these events to happen, but for Noah it is history, the waiting is over, but one day in some generation to come the Rapture, the supper in heaven, the tribulation, Armageddon, the millennium, and the destruction of Satan will be over. This Is why God said watch and wait.

Matthew 24:42, "Watch therefore: for ye know not what hour your Lord doth come."

Luke 12:37, "Blessed are those servants, whom the lord when he cometh shall find watching verily I say unto you, that he shall gird himself, and make them to sit down to meat, and will come forth and serve them." This is what I am looking forward to because either by grave or by rapture, if I am alive in that generation, I will be waiting, watching, and be about my Father business as Jesus said, to be ready for his coming.

Luke 2:49, "And he said unto them, how is it that ye sought me? wist ye not that I must be about my father's business?"

John 18:36, "Jesus answered, my kingdom is not of this world: if my kingdom were of this world, then would my servants fight, that I should not be delivered to the Jews: but now is my kingdom not from hence."

This picture of the Ark floating, like I said already, is a picture of the Kingdom of God, where Jesus is and where he will reign.

This is what he meant when he said in John 15:19, "If ye were of the world, the world would love his own: but because ye are not of the world, but I have chosen you out of the world, therefore the world hated you."

I remember when I heard the words, John 15:15–16

> [15]Henceforth I call you not servants; for the servant knewest not what his lord doeth: but I have called you friends; for all things that I have heard of my Father I have made known unto you. [16]Ye have not chosen me, but I have chosen you, and ordained you, that ye should go and bring forth fruit, and that your fruit should remain that whatsoever ye shall ask of the Father in my name, he may give it you.

Everyone at that supper table of the Lamb is chosen by God—period.

For instance, I was chosen in this world to represent God while I am here because he got something for everyone, he has chosen to do here on earth till we are at that place in Noah's days, while the Ark is floating, waiting on the water to recede back into the earth.

Others and I, when caught up in the Rapture, will to be waiting to go back to earth after the seven years come to an end, but meanwhile we have the Kingdom of God for now, while things are going on earth.

I could not unsee this when it was revealed to me.

When God put Adam in a deep sleep and took the rib from his side to create him a woman, helpmate, and his bride to be his wife, this was also a picture of the Rapture, because when Jesus died on the cross, as I have said earlier in this book, it was a deep sleep. And when the soldier pierced his side and water and blood came out, that was his spiritual rib, to make his bride and wife to be. This is the Church and bride that is carried to Jesus by God to the Son for the marriage, and that will happen when the Rapture takes place and everyone is called up, the dead in Christ Jesus first and then those who are alive.

Adam has already got Eve, but Jesus has not got his bride yet, but when the last born-again child of God is saved and the Church is called up to glory with Jesus he will have his bride, the Church.

Genesis 2:21, And the Lord God caused a deep sleep to fall upon Adam, and he slept: and he took one of his ribs, and closed up the flesh instead thereof."

John 19:34, "But one of the soldiers with a spear pierced his side, and forthwith came there out blood and water."

Genesis 2:22, "And the rib, which the Lord God had taken from man, made he a woman, and brought her unto the man."

The bride of Jesus Christ is still being formed, and when she is completed, our Father will take her to Jesus, just like he did with Eve. Again this is a picture of a grace period we are looking forward to.

On earth Satan is building his kingdom so that he can have that final battle with God to place his kingdom and overthrow God's kingdom; again, I could not unsee what the Lord had shown me.

God had created everything from earth that was not in the sky or the universe; in other words, he created heaven and earth, and everything else came out of the earth, even humankind.

Satan is going to imitate that: he is going to create his kingdom. He is going to go as far as to create life-forms, he is going to imitate creating humankind, and just like God created Adam from dust, Satan will create his life-form from earth as well.

Those that miss the Rapture in that generation will see this; unfortunately, it is not going to be good; it is not going to be freedom of choice; it is not going to be mercy anywhere. It is going to be the worst time in humankind's history, and I cannot unsee what I have seen through the Scriptures as revealed to me by the Holy Spirit.

Humankind is made up of three things: body, soul, and mind; in other words, this is the trinity of humankind's makeup; it takes all three items to create a person.

The body is the temple or housing of the soul, made from dirt of the earth.

The mind is the memory bank and stores all data about the person and does all the learning and growing in wisdom, knowledge, and understanding.

The soul is what uses both the mind and the body as they are needed. God gave to humankind a living soul.

Even Jesus's body and mind had to be humble and grow likewise.

This is why humankind has to be born again because Satan murders humankind's soul; it is dead, but not the body, and unless the individual takes the gift that God offers to restore their soul, they will not taste the second death that is eternity and the bottom pit that was made for Satan and his angels.

Satan knew that humankind's soul could not get back to heaven or God's presence. If he deceived Adam and Eve to lead them to sin, this was the first act of war toward God from Satan, but then God put a pause on everything and told humankind to do this type of sacrifice till the woman's seed comes to pass and cause the wrong to be right. Basically, this is separating the wheat from the tares or the righteous from the unrighteous, and what makes one righteous is not oneself but the idea of obedience toward God, and what he has to offer for the payment of the wages of sins that is owed from humankind since the Old Testament, which depended on the sacrifice that they gave unto God, the best of the best of what they had, and likewise in the New Testament, is depending on the one that paid our sins and the wages we owed, and that's Jesus Christ, the Son of God.

Satan knows he won that battle, not the war. That is why the flood happened, because the next attack did not work; he thought killing Abel would stop the woman's seed, but it did not. So he decided to contaminate humankind's bloodline so that the woman's seed would not be any threat to him.

These angels left their first estate to try to pollute and contaminate the human bloodline so that the seed of the woman would not be able to come forth. This is why God had to intervene to stop the contamination and preserve the pure bloodline. This was Satan's third battle, and he lost this one as well.

Genesis 3:15, "And I will put enmity between thee and the woman, and between thy seed and her seed; it shall bruise thy head, and thou shalt bruise his heel."

Luke 2:52, "And Jesus increased in wisdom and stature, and in favor with God and man."

2 Timothy 2:15, "Study to shew thyself approved unto God, a workman that needeth not to be ashamed, rightly dividing the word of truth."

Romans 12:2, "And be not conformed to this world: but be ye transformed by the renewing of your mind, that ye may prove what is that good, and acceptable, and perfect, will of God."

Satan has more battles all the way up to the cross, trying to stop the seed of the woman. His last battle concerning stopping the seed of the woman was in Matthew 4:1–11:

> [1]Then was Jesus led up of the Spirit into the wilderness to be tempted of the devil. [2]And when he had fasted forty days and forty nights, he was afterward hungered. [3]And when the tempter came to him, he said, if thou be the Son of God, command that these stones be made bread. [4]But he answered and said, it is written, Man shall not live by bread alone, but by every word that proceeded out of the mouth of God. [5]Then the devil taketh him up into the holy city, and setteth him on a pinnacle of the temple, [6]And saith unto him, If thou be the Son of God, cast thyself down: for it is written, He shall give his angels charge concerning thee: and in their hands they shall bear thee up, lest at any time thou dash thy foot against a stone. [7]Jesus said unto him, it is written again, thou shalt not tempt the Lord thy God. [8]Again, the devil taketh him up into an exceeding high mountain, and sheweth him all the kingdoms of the world, and the glory of them; [9]And saith unto him, all these things will I give thee, if thou wilt fall down and worship me. [10]Then saith Jesus

unto him, get thee hence, Satan: for it is written, thou shalt worship the Lord thy God, and him only shalt thou serve. [11]Then the devil leaveth him, and behold, angels came and ministered unto him.

Where Adam failed, Jesus was triumphant and victorious against Satan's temptation toward him, but when Jesus got to the cross and gave up his ghost and said it was finished, he was literally talking about the wages of sin that all of humankind owed.

Satan now knows that the only thing he can do now is to bring disbelief to everything that is Christlike and build his kingdom; this is why it said in 2 Thessalonians 2:11–12, "[11]And for this cause God shall send them strong delusion, that they should believe a lie: [12]That they all might be damned who believed not the truth, but had pleasure in unrighteousness."

They are not going to give up their pleasure. That generation of the tribulation compared in the days I am living, I can only imagine how many times worst it will be compared to my days.

Satan knows his time is short, so he has been working hard on his kingdom. From the time Jesus died and gave up his ghost, Satan has been working hard ever since to this present day to get his kingdom where he needs it to be, and he definitely is going to have an army.

Satan's life-form will be a trinity as well: body, demon, and brain.

The body will be from earth as well: all the materials that are gathered from the earth to create metal substances, soft substances, or anything that can make a body. The body will most likely be a robot, and the robot will mostly look like a human; it will be hard to tell the difference. These robots are to house the demons, which will operate the body like a human soul operates their body. The brain will be computer chips. The size of the information, instructions, or capability will allow the robot to do whatever is programmed on the main brain.

The demon is like the soul in the human body. It will use the robot and brain to its advantage.

This is what Satan is building to form his kingdom.

Picture pharaoh the king, his soldiers and the Hebrew children's. Now picture pharaoh as Satan and his soldiers as his fallen angels as robots and the Hebrew's children as humankind.

Exodus 5:17–19

> [17]But he said, Ye are idle, ye are idle: therefore ye say, let us go and do sacrifice to the Lord. [18]Go therefore now, and work; for there shall no straw be given you, yet shall ye deliver the tale of bricks. [19]And the officers of the children of Israel did see that they were in evil case, after it was said, Ye shall not minish ought from your bricks of your daily task.

The Lord said work while it is day; the night is coming, when no man can work; this is why he said that. It also refers to death.

John 9:4, "I must work the works of him that sent me, while it is day: the night cometh, when no man can work."

This generation during the tribulation will be under Satan's government, and everything done will be for him, and his soldiers will enforce his laws and rules without mercy.

Humankind will be nothing more than slaves to him, and that will be a lot of work for those slaves to do because someone has to keep these robots and machines in good shape and ready and perform maintenance or whatever else needs to be done.

Elon Musk, talking about AI, said that it was dangerous for humankind to pursue automated intelligence because it would eventually take over humankind.

The Lord had already revealed this to me long before Elon Musk was brought to my attention, and what the Lord was showing me and what he was saying was confirmation.

Scientists are already at the point of having perfect robots, looking just like male or female humans, able to have emotions, with reactions that mimic humans.' All I had to do was look at different articles and videos to see that it was really happening. This is the other reason that God must destroy everything again because he cannot allow Satan, his army of robots, and those that are marked of the beast to take over his creation and then enslave humankind and take God completely out of the picture and the very thing that he created.

Revelation 13:15–18

> [15]And he had power to give life unto the image of the beast, that the image of the beast should both speak, and cause that as many as would not worship the image of the beast should be killed. [16]And he causes all, both small and great, rich and poor, free and bond, to receive a mark in their right hand, or in their foreheads: [17]And that no man might buy or sell, save he that had the mark, or the name of the beast, or the number of his name.

Revelation 16:13, "And I saw three unclean spirits like frogs come out of the mouth of the dragon, and out of the mouth of the beast, and out of the mouth of the false prophet."

Satan is going to imitate God on his ability to be everywhere at the same time and know everything that is going on and when it is going on, and the only way Satan can imitate this is putting an electronic computer chip in every human being. This is why if you do not take the mark, you will be killed.

What this does is put Satan as a god to those on earth or take the mark of the beast. When one takes the mark of the beast, that person is becoming one with Satan, like when one becomes one with the Lord by the Holy Ghost, except that Satan is connected to him by way of a chip being put in your skin on some part of your body. Which is an imitation of the Holy Ghost that seal God's chosen people. This chip the mark of the beast will be an imitation of God omnipotent for Satan to appear to be omnipotent.

Revelation 7:14–17

> [14]And I said unto him, Sir, thou knewest. And he said to me, these are they which came out of great tribulation, and

have washed their robes, and made them white in the blood of the Lamb. [15]Therefore are they before the throne of God, and serve him day and night in his temple: and he that sited on the throne shall dwell among them. [16]They shall hunger no more, neither thirst anymore; neither shall the sun light on them, nor any heat. [17]For the Lamb which is in the midst of the throne shall feed them, and shall lead them unto living fountains of waters: and God shall wipe away all tears from their eyes.

This is what has to be done to make it through the tribulation: simply refuse the mark of the beast and go through whatever an individual will have to go through; during this time, this will be how you can wash your garments white in the blood of the Lamb.

Genesis 41:53–54

[53]And the seven years of plenteousness, that was in the land of Egypt, were ended. [54]And the seven years of dearth began to come, according as Joseph had said: and the dearth was in all lands; but in all the land of Egypt there was bread.

Daniel 4:25

That they shall drive thee from men, and thy dwelling shall be with the beasts of the field, and they shall make thee to eat grass as oxen, and they shall wet thee with the dew of heaven, and seven times shall pass over thee, till thou know that the most High ruleth in the kingdom of men, and giveth it to whomsoever he will.

These two stories both deal with plagues lasting seven years. One was able to store up, while in the tribulation there will be no storing up, unless it is already in the individual's possession, as long as the individual does not take the mark.

Nebuchadnezzar living in the wilderness is more of a picture of those that refuse the mark, surviving the best that the individual can do and being undetected by any government officials in the tribulation period.

Luke 16:20–22

> [20]And there was a certain beggar named Lazarus, which was laid at his gate, full of sores, [21]And desiring to be fed with the crumbs which fell from the rich man's table: moreover the dogs came and licked his sores. [22]And it came to pass, that the beggar died, and was carried by the angels into Abraham's bosom: the rich man also died, and was buried.

There might be some that do not see this as a beautiful picture, but those during the tribulation will, because this is what they would most likely be going through. There will be no one to help, and they will not be able to buy, sell, trade, or get medical help, to the point they die over the mark that was not taken and carried to the Lord or if possible, lived through the seven-year tribulation without taking the mark.

There are two kingdoms being established, one in heaven, one on earth, one is God's and one Satan's claiming godship.

Satan is saying, whatever God does I can do better, like making humankind. In Satan's mind humankind is useless, their expiration date could be between birth to at least 120 years, they cannot be controlled, but they are able to be manipulated by their own emotions, especially greed, lust, and thirst of power or any other desires the flesh wants. Satan and his followers need a body they can control. When I look at them trying to control some individual, they have a process. That individual, according to the records of the Scriptures most of the time is violent, harmful, and a danger to themselves as well as others.

Mark 5:1–20 [1]And they came over unto the other side of the sea, into the country of the Gadarenes. [2]And when he was come out of the ship, immediately there met him out of the tombs a man with an unclean spirit, [3]Who had his dwelling among the tombs; and no man could bind him, no, not with chains: [4]Because that he had been often bound with fetters and chains, and the chains had been plucked asunder by him, and the fetters broken in pieces: neither could any man tame him. [5]And always, night and day, he was in the mountains, and in the tombs, crying, and cutting himself with stones. [6]But when he saw Jesus afar off, he ran and worshipped him, [7]And cried with a loud voice, and said, what have I to do with thee, Jesus, thou Son of the most high God? I adjure thee by God, that thou torment me not. [8]For he said unto him, Come out of the man, thou unclean spirit. [9]And he asked him, what is thy name? And he answered, saying, my name is Legion: for we are many. [10]And he besought him much that he would not send them away out of the country. [11]Now there was there nigh unto the mountains a great herd of swine feeding. [12]And all the devils besought him, saying, send us into the swine, that we may enter into them. [13]And forthwith Jesus gave them leave. And the unclean spirits went out, and entered into the swine: and the herd ran violently down a steep place into the sea, (they were about two thousand;) and were choked in the sea. [14]And they that fed the swine fled, and told it in the city, and in the country. And they went out to see what it was that was done. [15]And they come to Jesus, and see him that was possessed with the devil, and had the legion, sitting, and clothed, and in his right mind: and they were afraid. [16]And they that saw it told them how it befell to him that was possessed with the devil, and also concerning the swine. [17]And they began to pray for him to depart out of their coasts. [18]And when he was come into the ship, he that had been possessed with the devil prayed him that he might be with him. [19]Howbeit Jesus suffered him not, but saith unto him, go home to thy friends, and tell them how great things the Lord hath done for thee, and hath had compassion on thee. [20]And he departed, and began to publish in Decapolis how great things Jesus had done for him: and all men did marvel.

The process is man is fighting the demons, and the demons are fighting him; there is no real control or benefit.

There is no benefit or gain for the demons, but God is getting glory for delivering the man from the demons and the man being delivered, which is good, but not for the demons.

Demons can give some ability to tell fortunes, conquer up spirits they can mute, to the point where you are not able to talk or other mental issues or physical issues, but the whole point is they want to have a host, they need a body.

With the technology that humankind has, I am able to see these plans come together, by social media, news media, or talk shows. It is coming together as Satan organizes for the seven-year reign that he will be allowed to have.

Matthew 16:23, "But he turned, and said unto Peter, get thee behind me, Satan: thou art an offence unto me: for thou severest not the things that be of God, but those that be of men."

Jesus knew it was Satan that put that thought into Peter's mind to speak. That is why Jesus said to the spirits and see whether they are of God or not.

1 John 4:1–5 [1]Beloved, believe not every spirit, but try the spirits whether they are of God: because many false prophets are gone out into the world. [2]Hereby know ye the Spirit of God: Every spirit that confessed that Jesus Christ is come in the flesh is of God: [3]And every spirit that confessed not that Jesus Christ is come in the flesh is not of God: and this is that spirit of antichrist, whereof ye have heard that it should come; and even now already is it in the world. [4]Ye are of God, little children, and have overcome them: because greater is he that is in you, than he that is in the world. [5]They are of the world: therefore speak they of the world, and the world heareth them.

Satan and his followers can put thoughts in an individual's mind, but it's up to the individual to sort out what is going through their mind because it's not always your own thoughts; it can be a spirit of God or the spirit of Satan whispering into your mind, and it's up to me to discern in my own mind whether it's of God or not, according to his Word, which it should line up with.

Revelation 13:15, "And he had power to give life unto the image of the beast, that the image of the beast should both speak, and cause that as many as would not worship the image of the beast should be killed."

I have heard that before. Yes, in Genesis 1:26:

> And God said, let us make man in our image, after our likeness: and let them have dominion over the fish of the sea, and over the fowl of the air, and over the cattle, and over all the earth, and over every creeping thing that crept upon the earth.

God made man in his image, and so did the beast; again, God made man and put a soul in man, gave man a mind, and gave humankind the ability to walk, think, and be put in charge over the worldly affairs and all that dwells in it.

The image of the beast is a robot, and it is in the image of its creator, and it too is not human.

God gave life to mankind, but the beast is giving life to a robot.

John saw what he thought was a statue, an image that came alive and was able to be like humanlike.

The image of the beast was given the power to speak and to have those that would not worship the image to be killed. Even though some will miss the Rapture, this is where they will be redeemed: the refusal of that mark is salvation and death, or their resurrection; in other words, the dragon, the beast, the prophet have laid claim of the entire world, which was meant for humankind, and this is another reason God has to put a stop to it because they're literally bringing humankind in submission and slavery for their purpose and goal. And if that generation does take the mark, they are automatically doomed, just like those outside the Ark of Noah's days, and those that refuse the mark will suffer death. Or if they are able to survive by hiding or avoiding the image of the beast, they will possibly suffer starvation and harsh weather conditions, sleeping wherever they can sleep, and there is so much more that they will endure.

Robots will be programmed to kill, put it this way. Humankind is over all creatures and is at the top of the food chain. Robots will be over humankind. And they will serve the dragon in his kingdom on earth.

Satan, by character, is not humble and will not live by faith or take a chance on the goals he has.

Satan is having humankind right now in my generation making robots. That will be his army, not humankind.

Humankind cannot stand against God or Satan in the flesh, but those in the spirit of the Lord can stand against the devil.

Robots can last longer, they will be more intelligent and reliable than humans, and they do not have a soul, so they have no conscience; they just do what they are programmed to do with no questions, while humans do not have the stability do be dependent on and the loyalty that Satan requires.

The mark of the beast is no different than cattle being branded to let others know who they belong to, or when Hitler marked the Jewish people with a tattoo of numbers on their hand, wrist, or arm, to be able to identify each one of the Jews.

Revelation 19:9, "And he saith unto me, Write, Blessed are they which are called unto the marriage supper of the Lamb. And he saith unto me, these are the true sayings of God."

I came to understand that the call to the marriage supper of the Lamb is the calling up of the believers in the grace period or the Rapture, as it is called as well. This is why God said blessed are they who are called unto the marriage supper of the Lamb, because they will miss the seven-year tribulation.

There is a reminder of this scripture in Matthew 25:1–13:

> [1]Then shall the kingdom of heaven be likened unto ten virgins, which took their lamps, and went forth to meet the bridegroom. [2]And five of them were wise, and five were foolish. [3]They that were foolish took their lamps, and took no oil with them: [4]But the wise took oil in their vessels with their lamps. [5]While the bridegroom tarried, they all slumbered and slept. [6]And at midnight there was a cry made, Behold, the bridegroom cometh; go ye out to meet him. [7]Then all those virgins arose, and trimmed their lamps. [8]And the foolish said unto the wise, give us of your oil; for our lamps are gone out. [9]But the wise answered, saying, not so; let there be not enough for us and you: but go ye rather to them that sell, and buy for yourselves. [10]And while they went to buy, the bridegroom came; and they that were ready went in with him to the marriage: and the door was shut. [11]Afterward came also the other virgins, saying, Lord, Lord,

open to us. [12]But he answered and said, Verily I say unto you, I know you not. [13]Watch therefore, for ye know neither the day nor the hour wherein the Son of man cometh.

This is talking about the Rapture as well with the ten virgins. It is time for the Lamb's marriage and supper. Five were left while five went in the Rapture. And the five that are ready are with the Lord with the supper table prepared for all called up in the Rapture. The five not ready for the Rapture are left behind to endure the events of the seven-year tribulation.

This is what Jesus was saying as well in Matthew 24:37–42: [37]But as the days of Noah were, so shall also the coming of the Son of man be. [38]For as in the days that were before the flood they were eating and drinking, marrying and giving in marriage, until the day that Noah entered into the ark, [39]And knew not until the flood came, and took them all away; so shall also the coming of the Son of man be. [40]Then shall two be in the field; the one shall be taken, and the other left. [41]Two women shall be grinding at the mill; the one shall be taken, and the other left. [42]Watch therefore: for ye know not what hour your Lord doth come.

The key here is being ready as a believer, because I want to be at the Lamb's marriage and supper table rather than in the seven-year tribulation. This will be different from the grace period before the Rapture.

The image of the beast has power from the beast, and the beast has power from the dragon.

The first beast was wounded. And people were amazed at his healing. The second beast came after. Scripture said that the first beast came out of the sea and the second out of the earth.

Those left behind or who missed the Rapture will be faced with these beasts that will make war with them, and their goal is the genocide of believers left behind.

Revelation 13:1, "And I stood upon the sand of the sea, and saw a beast rise up out of the sea, having seven heads and ten horns, and upon his horns ten crowns, and upon his heads the name of blasphemy."

Revelation 13:11, "And I beheld another beast coming up out of the earth; and he had two horns like a lamb, and he spake as a dragon."

Revelation 13:7, "And it was given unto him to make war with the saints, and to overcome them: and power was given him over all kindreds, and tongues, and nations."

War is to make everyone worship the dragon, the image of the beast, and take the mark.

Revelation 13:8, "And all that dwell upon the earth shall worship him, whose names are not written in the book of life of the Lamb slain from the foundation of the world."

The first beast has 42 months to get things in order for the dragon and get rid of the Word of God and all those who still believe in God even though they have missed the Rapture because most know that they are still able to make it as long as they do not take the mark of the beast.

Revelation 13:5, "And there was given unto him a mouth speaking great things and blasphemies; and power was given unto him to continue forty and two months."

Revelation 7:13–14

> [13]And one of the elders answered, saying unto me, What are these which are arrayed in white robes? and whence came they? [14]And I said unto him, Sir, thou knowest. And he said to me, these are they which came out of great tribulation, and have washed their robes, and made them white in the blood of the Lamb.

Revelation 20:4

> And I saw thrones, and they sat upon them, and judgment was given unto them: and I saw the souls of them that were beheaded for the witness of Jesus, and for the word of God, and which had not worshipped the beast, neither his image, neither had received his mark upon their foreheads, or in their hands; and they lived and reigned with Christ a thousand years.

These two scriptures are talking about the same souls or people. These people have decided no matter what, they were not going to take the mark or worship anything or anyone other than God. No matter what the cost, which would be beheading or a worst torture.

Daniel 3:15–18 [15]Now if ye be ready that at what time ye hear the sound of the cornet, flute, harp, sackbut, psaltery, and dulcimer, and all kinds of music, ye fall down and worship the image which I have made; well: but if ye worship not, ye shall be cast the same hour into the midst of a burning fiery furnace; and who is that God that shall deliver you out of my hands? [16]Shadrach, Meshach, and Abednego, answered and said to the king, O Nebuchadnezzar, we are not careful to answer thee in this matter. [17]If it be so, our God whom we serve is able to deliver us from the burning fiery furnace, and he will deliver us out of thine hand, O king. [18]But if not, be it known unto thee, O king, that we will not serve thy gods, nor worship the golden image which thou hast set up.

The only difference in these Hebrew brothers and those in the tribulation is that there was only three that stood up against this ungodly command, while in the tribulation there will be untold multiple people that will as well, but these Hebrew brothers were delivered from the furnace. For the generation in the tribulation days, their death will be the deliverance.

One thing that has not changed from the grace period to the tribulation period is the sins of the world have been paid in full; this has not and will not change.

The whole point of the tribulation is twofold: to get as many souls as God is able to, and to destroy those whose names are not written in the Book of Life.

Revelation 16:9, "And men were scorched with great heat, and blasphemed the name of God, which hath power over these plagues: and they repented not to give him glory."

God in all his righteousness, patience, long-suffering, gentleness, kindness, and as lover of his creation is trying to reach out to as many people as he can in these last days of the tribulation.

Daniel 4 with the event of nebuchadnezzar reminded me of what was going on in revelation 16:9. That is all that God was throwing at him, but at some time nebuchadnezzar knew God, and he understood why all these things were happening, and at some point he does repent and does have a change of heart even to the point that he wrote Daniel in the third person, as though he was not the same person he was writing about, but these men in the tribulation would neither repent nor turn to God but rather take the wrath of God.

The Lamb's supper is going on as the tribulation is happening. The difference is there is a reunion, rejoicing, and fellowshipping. Seeing what eyes have not seen, hearing what ears have not heard, and just having a glorious time in the Lord, but on the other hand, you got destruction, death, chaos, and just a terrible time in humankind's history like never before.

1 Corinthians 2:9, "But as it is written, Eye hath not seen, nor ear heard, neither have entered into the heart of man, the things which God hath prepared for them that love him."

Isaiah 64:4, "For since the beginning of the world men have not heard, nor perceived by the ear, neither hath the eye seen, O God, beside thee, what he hath prepared for him that waiteth for him."

2 Peter 3:9, "The Lord is not slack concerning his promise, as some men count slackness; but is longsuffering to us-ward, not willing that any should perish, but that all should come to repentance."

God's character is so awesome that he takes up the body of Christ Jesus. And while the Lamb's supper is going on he is still reaching out to get as many souls as he can.

The whole time he is separating the wheat from the tares, but God is so thoughtful that he wants even to separate a wheat that is tangled in with the tare.

God is like a gold miner who is looking for those last gold nuggets. He takes the gold pan, dips it in the sand, clay, or dirt, and rinses the unwounded dirt and rocks to the point it only sees the gold nuggets and then takes them and puts them aside to be kept for his treasures.

The seven-year tribulation is what God is doing, getting everyone that misses the Rapture. He is getting the remaining wheat that will have to suffer and be killed as a response to not taking the mark of the beast or worshipping the beast.

MATTHEW 25:1-13

[1]Then shall the kingdom of heaven be likened unto ten virgins, which took their lamps, and went forth to meet the bridegroom. [2]And five of them were wise, and five were foolish. [3]They that were foolish took their lamps, and took no oil with them: [4]But the wise took oil in their vessels with their lamps. [5]While the bridegroom tarried, they all slumbered and slept. [6]And at midnight there was a cry made, Behold, the bridegroom cometh; go ye out to meet him. [7]Then all those virgins arose, and trimmed their lamps. [8]And the foolish said unto the wise, Give us of your oil; for our lamps are gone out. [9]But the wise answered, saying, Not so; let there be not enough for us and you: but go ye rather to them that sell, and buy for yourselves. [10]And while they went to buy, the bridegroom came; and they that were ready went in with him to the marriage: and the door was shut. [11]Afterward came also the other virgins, saying, Lord, Lord, open to us. [12]But he answered and said, Verily I say unto you, I know you not. [13]Watch therefore, for ye know neither the day nor the hour wherein the Son of man cometh.

The foolish can not go in the rupture, but will be able to be part of the kingdom of God by refusing the mark of the beast and not worshipping the image of the beast.

This parable of the ten virgins said five were barely ready and five was not ready he did not say that they would not all ten be in the kingdom of God, but that half missed the rapture, and the other half got to go in the rapture. The half that missed the rapture will have to endure the tribulation to make it to the kingdom of God.

This made me think of a debate in the religious realm about the pre tribulation and mid tribulation their both right and do not know it.

I understand clearly how important it is to be ready when the Rapture takes place and avoid the seven-year tribulation, if I was in that generation, but it is the same as death, Rapture, or seven-year tribulation.

I came to understand how to do that. As the scriptures said in Matthew 24:42, "Watch therefore: for ye know not what hour your Lord doth come."

Matthew 26:41, "Watch and pray, that ye enter not into temptation: the spirit indeed is willing, but the flesh is weak."

1 Corinthians 16:13, "Watch ye, stand fast in the faith, quit you like men, be strong."

There are snares the devil knows how to set to get someone trapped in. No different from a hunter, because he is like a roaring lion ready to catch anyone he can. Something so simple and innocent to the eyes and mind can be the snare that can grab someone to cause them to take their eyes off the Lord.

1 Peter 5:8, "Be sober, be vigilant; because your adversary the devil, as a roaring lion, walketh about, seeking whom he may devour."

Satan has no power over no one, except those that choose to let him have that power.

Satan has the same agenda in the grace period or the seven-year tribulation. That is preventing souls from getting back to the Lord.

He will use fear, greed, power, and pleasure of the flesh, instead of contentment, thankfulness, trust, and obedience to God.

These scriptures give insight to what Satan and his fallen angels do to keep that relationship from an individual and God.

2 Corinthians 11:14, "And no marvel; for Satan himself is transformed into an angel of light."

Luke 22:31, "And the Lord said, Simon, Simon, behold, Satan hath desired to have you, that he may sift you as wheat."

This is why a child of God needs to depend on the Holy Spirit and the Word of God. And this is why the scripture said this in 1 John 4:4, "Ye are of God, little children, and have overcome them: because greater is he that is in you, than he that is in the world."

The child of God's powers is who is in him, the Holy Ghost, and he is the key to getting and being ready for the Rapture and to be able to sit at the Lamb's supper table.

John 14:26, "But the Comforter, which is the Holy Ghost, whom the Father will send in my name, he shall teach you all things, and bring all things to your remembrance, whatsoever I have said unto you."

John 16:7, "Nevertheless I tell you the truth; It is expedient for you that I go away: for if I go not away, the Comforter will not come unto you; but if I depart, I will send him unto you."

John 15:26, "But when the Comforter is come, whom I will send unto you from the Father, even the Spirit of truth, which proceeded from the Father, he shall testify of me."

John 16:13

> Howbeit when he, the Spirit of truth, is come, he will guide you into all truth: for he shall not speak of himself; but whatsoever he shall hear, that shall he speak, and he will shew you things to come.

Romans 8:26, "Likewise the Spirit also helpeth our infirmities: for we know not what we should pray for as we ought: but the Spirit itself maketh intercession for us with groanings which cannot be uttered."

This is why so many people have a hard time understanding the Word of God, because they are trying to understand the Word of God without the Holy Ghost.

I have come to understand that the Word of God was written by men that the Holy Ghost moved on to write the Word of God, so it only makes sense to allow the Holy Ghost to help me understand it.

2 Peter 1:21, "For the prophecy came not in old time by the will of man: but holy men of God spake as they were moved by the Holy Ghost."

The point is that a child of God is nothing without the Holy Ghost in them. And the only way to get the Holy Ghost is believing that the Son of God died for humankind's wages of sins. This is the gift of God.

This is for the grace period as the Holy Ghost gets the children ready for the Rapture to go to the Lamb's supper, but those that are in the tribulation will suffer, because Satan will be allowed to govern the world for seven years, cleaning it from anything that is a reminder of God and his Word and anyone that still wants to believe in God or Jesus, his Son.

The Lamb's supper is going on, and the tribulation is taking place at the same time.

Satan's kingdom is being built on earth, and he is getting his soldiers to gather his slaves because he believes that his kingdom will overcome God's kingdom.

God is allowing Satan to believe that and is allowing him to clean out the remaining wheat or believers from earth so he can control everything with the AI that he has, which is imitating building life as God did, as I said earlier. And with the mark, Satan will also imitate God's omnipresence.

Satan will know where an individual is at all times, what they own, what they do for a living. That mark of the beast is an imitation of the Holy Ghost being in a child of God, but in a child of the devil, because once marked, there is no turning back; these individuals are doomed just as much as the dragon, beast, and the false prophet are.

CHAPTER 6

THE DOVE AND THE OLIVE LEAF

The dove and the olive leaf show how powerful God is, though he does not need to prove his power, but his gentleness and humbleness allow him too.

Genesis 8:11, "And the dove came into him in the evening; and, lo, in her mouth was an olive leaf pluckt off: so Noah knew that the waters were abated from off the earth."

The dove is a picture of the Holy Ghost, and the olive leaf is a picture of the two last witnesses in the seven-year tribulation being brought back to the body of Christ Jesus being resurrected after they were killed and laid on the street for three and a half days.

The Holy Ghost is like a dove when he rests on Jesus when John baptized him.

John 1:32–33

> [32]And John bare record, saying, I saw the Spirit descending from heaven like a dove, and it abode upon him. [33]And I knew him not: but he that sent me to baptize with water, the same said unto me, Upon whom thou shalt see the Spirit descending, and remaining on him, the same is he which baptizeth with the Holy Ghost.

Revelation 11:11–12

> [11]And after three days and a half the spirit of life from God entered into them, and they stood upon their feet; and great fear fell upon them which saw them. [12]And they heard a

great voice from heaven saying unto them, Come up hither. And they ascended up to heaven in a cloud; and their enemies beheld them.

There are two missing from the body of Christ Jesus during the Rapture and the gathering of the saints with Jesus and being with Jesus. And this is a picture of them returning back to the body of Jesus Christ after doing what God sent them to do during the tribulation.

I have come to understand that the two witness are not what I was taught to be, which was Enoch, Elijah or moses but rather Israel with the 144,000 that will be saved and marked in the forehead belonging to the Lord and savior and America God's chosen nation United States of America in which he used to fulfill that which Israel was supposed to have done for God as being a light and blessing to other nation but in the tribulation both will be a light to all nation until God allow Satan to declare war on these two nation or prophets because Israel and The United States of America has the word of God Israel is a picture of the Old Testament United States of America is the picture of the New Testament the grace period. But now the rapture is over, and they are both in the tribulation period warring against the beast and what done to them the same is return back to the attacker after three and a half years of this God will allow this to nation be defeated and the world will rejoice over their defeat.

Revelation 11:4, "These are the two olive trees, and the two candlesticks standing before the God of the earth."

Zechariah 4:12–14

> [12]And I answered again, and said unto him, What be these two olive branches which through the two golden pipes empty the golden oil out of themselves? [13]And he answered me and said, Knowest thou not what these be? And I said, No, my lord. [14]Then said he, These are the two anointed ones, that stand by the LORD of the whole earth.

The two nations have been preserved till they are needed in the first three and a half years in the seven-year tribulation and get the remaining souls to warn those of that generation not to take the mark of beast and turn to God unto death, which many will refuse the mark unto death.

Genesis 5:22–24

> [22]And Enoch walked with God after he begat Methuselah three hundred years, and begat sons and daughters: [23]And all the days of Enoch were three hundred sixty and five years: [24]And Enoch walked with God: and he was not; for God took him.

2 Kings 2:1, "And it came to pass, when the Lord would take up Elijah into heaven by a whirlwind, that Elijah went with Elisha from Gilgal."

2 Kings 2:11–12

> [11]And it came to pass, as they still went on, and talked, that, behold, there appeared a chariot of fire, and horses of fire, and parted them both asunder; and Elijah went up by a whirlwind into heaven. [12]And Elisha saw it, and he cried, My father, my father, the chariot of Israel, and the horsemen thereof. And he saw him no more: and he took hold of his own clothes, and rent them in two pieces.

The three I was taught to believe was Enoch and Elijah cause they did not taste death and moses because no one knows where he is buried as for moses it appointed once for man to die. And as for Enoch and Elijah flesh can not enter the kingdom of God.

1 CORINTHIANS 15:50

Now this I say, brethren, that flesh and blood cannot inherit the kingdom of God; neither doth corruption inherit incorruption.

The scripture said in Hebrews 9:27–28

> [27]And as it is appointed unto men once to die, but after this the judgment: [28]So Christ was once offered to bear the sins of many; and unto them that look for him shall he appear the second time without sin unto salvation.

The two nations has their citizen dead in the street, and God put life back in them; it is their resurrection. And is their return back to the body of Christ Jesus, and the marriage of the Lamb can take place; until then the rest of the body is fellowshipping, having a banquet and just enjoying being in the presence of God and the Lamb of God, as these two nation will be fighting against Satan world order and his system of his will on the world. For the first three and half years till God allow them to be defeated.

Revelation 11:1–13

> [1]And there was given me a reed like unto a rod: and the angel stood, saying, Rise, and measure the temple of God, and the altar, and them that worship therein. [2]But the court which is without the temple leave out, and measure it not; for it is given unto the Gentiles: and the holy city shall they tread under foot forty and two months. [3]And I will give power unto my two witnesses, and they shall prophesy a thousand two hundred and threescore days, clothed in sackcloth. [4]These are the two olive trees, and the two candlesticks standing before the God of the earth. [5]And if any man will hurt them, fire proceedeth out of their mouth, and devoureth their enemies: and if any man will hurt them, he must in this manner be killed. [6]These have power to shut heaven, that it rain not in the days of their prophecy: and have power over waters to turn them to blood, and to smite the earth with all plagues, as often as they will. [7]And when they shall have finished their testimony, the beast that ascendeth out of the bottomless pit shall make war against them, and shall overcome them, and kill them. [8]And their dead bodies shall lie in the street of the great city, which spiritually is called Sodom and Egypt, where also our Lord was crucified. [9]And they of the people and kindreds and tongues and nations shall see their dead bodies three days and an half, and shall not suffer their dead bodies to be put in graves. [10]And they that dwell upon the earth shall rejoice over them, and make merry, and shall send gifts one to another; because these two prophets tormented them that

dwelt on the earth. [11]And after three days and an half the spirit of life from God entered into them, and they stood upon their feet; and great fear fell upon them which saw them. [12]And they heard a great voice from heaven saying unto them, Come up hither. And they ascended up to heaven in a cloud; and their enemies beheld them. [13]And the same hour was there a great earthquake, and the tenth part of the city fell, and in the earthquake were slain of men seven thousand: and the remnant were affrighted, and gave glory to the God of heaven.

God said in Genesis 8:21

And the Lord smelled a sweet savour; and the Lord said in his heart, I will not again curse the ground any more for man's sake; for the imagination of man's heart is evil from his youth; neither will I again smite any more everything living, as I have done."

That sweet savor God smelled is the picture of his son Jesus and his righteousness that is coming sometime in the future and is going to pay the debt of the wages of sin for humankind with his death.

God got me to understand that what his Son Jesus did at Calvary paid off the debt of all sins once and for all; there are no more payments needed, and no more sacrifice is needed.

I pay someone's debt of a billion dollars' mansion, and I tell that someone it is paid for and taken care of, go on about your life without this debt anymore.

This is what Jesus the Son of God did for my sins and the sins of the whole world. There is no more debt of sins.

If someone's mansion got paid for but they are still worrying on how to make a payment, that does not change the fact that it is paid for. This someone simply just does not believe it is paid for.

Jesus paid the wages of my sins, not mine alone, but everyone is that was ever born into this world. Just because I or anyone goes around and worries about sins and is concerned about going to hell and just does not believe their sins are paid for or doubts it is paid for does not change the fact that all sins, past, present, and future, are paid off in full.

The just is to live by faith and not by sight according to Romans 1:17, "For therein is the righteousness of God revealed from faith to faith: as it is written, The just shall live by faith."

Galatians 3:11, "But that no man is justified by the law in the sight of God, it is evident: for, The just shall live by faith."

Hebrews 10:38, "Now the just shall live by faith: but if any man draw back, my soul shall have no pleasure in him."

Doubting is the opposite of faith. Believing is very important; it is unbelief that sends one to hell, not sin.

Genesis 8:21

> And the Lord smelled a sweet savour; and the Lord said in his heart, I will not again curse the ground any more for man's sake; for the imagination of man's heart is evil from his youth; neither will I again smite any more everything living, as I have done.

God just does not kill, because he can and has the power too. If so, humankind would have been destroyed completely already by now.

Nahum 1:3, "The Lord is slow to anger, and great in power, and will not at all acquit the wicked: the Lord hath his way in the whirlwind and in the storm, and the clouds are the dust of his feet."

Psalms 103:8, "The Lord is merciful and gracious, slow to anger, and plenteous in mercy."

Jonah 4:2

> And he prayed unto the Lord, and said, I pray thee, O Lord, was not this my saying, when I was yet in my country? Therefore I fled before unto Tarshish: for I knew that thou

art a gracious God, and merciful, slow to anger, and of great kindness, and repentest thee of the evil.

2 Peter 3:9, "The Lord is not slack concerning his promise, as some men count slackness; but is longsuffering to us-ward, not willing that any should perish, but that all should come to repentance."

God to get to the point that his anger is revealed. His anger is not quick and sudden or spontaneous. Whatever it was that caused God's anger has went on for some time, because he will warn anyone what would happen to a person way before he gets to the point of anger, but when God does get to that point, then action will be taken.

Jonah 1:1–2, "[1]Now the word of the Lord came unto Jonah the son of Amittai, saying, [2]Arise, go to Nineveh, that great city, and cry against it; for their wickedness is come up before me."

Revelation 2:4–6

[4]Nevertheless I have somewhat against thee, because thou hast left thy first love. [5]Remember therefore from whence thou art fallen, and repent, and do the first works; or else I will come unto thee quickly, and will remove thy candlestick out of his place, except thou repent. [6]But this thou hast, that thou hatest the deeds of the Nicolaitanes, which I also hate.

Ezekiel 3:17–18

[17]Son of man, I have made thee a watchman unto the house of Israel: therefore hear the word at my mouth, and give them warning from me. [18]When I say unto the wicked, Thou shalt surely die; and thou givest him not warning, nor speakest to warn the wicked from his wicked way, to save his life; the same wicked man shall die in his iniquity; but his blood will I require at thine hand.

1 Kings 13:8–9

[8]And the man of God said unto the king, If thou wilt give me half thine house, I will not go in with thee, neither will I eat bread nor drink water in this place: [9]For so was it charged

me by the word of the Lord, saying, Eat no bread, nor drink water, nor turn again by the same way that thou camest.

The three and half years of the tribulation are still showing God long-suffering, patience, and that he is slow to anger, by allowing the two nations to prophecy and warn the people of that generation and to reach as many as they could, before they would take the mark of the beast and seal their fate forever. This really shows the kindness and mercy of God reaching out to the last ones that will receive eternal life, by refusing the mark, suffering, and sometimes being killed and not suffer to be part of the second death.

The grace period is over now, and there is no more turning of the cheek. It is more like in the Old Testament, an eye for an eye, because the two nations are to do unto those the same way to which they are done. Make me think of do unto others as you would want them to do unto you, but now it is the opposite. They are to do unto them as they do to them. Except they do it with fire. Which is missile coming out of chambers that appear to look like a mouth has open up and fire came out.

Revelation 11:3–5 ³And I will give power unto my two witnesses, and they shall prophesy a thousand two hundred and threescore days, clothed in sackcloth. ⁴These are the two olive trees, and the two candlesticks standing before the God of the earth. ⁵And if any man will hurt them, fire proceedeth out of their mouth, and devoureth their enemies: and if any man will hurt them, he must in this manner be killed.

Matthew 7:12, "Therefore all things whatsoever ye would that men should do to you, do ye even so to them: for this is the law and the prophets."

Exodus 21:23–27

> ²³And if any mischief follow, then thou shalt give life for life, ²⁴Eye for eye, tooth for tooth, hand for hand, foot for foot, ²⁵Burning for burning, wound for wound, stripe for stripe. ²⁶And if a man smite the eye of his servant, or the eye of his maid, that it perish; he shall let him go free for his eye's sake. ²⁷And if he smite out his manservant's tooth,

or his maidservant's tooth; he shall let him go free for his tooth's sake.

Matthew 5:38–39

> [38]Ye have heard that it hath been said, An eye for an eye, and a tooth for a tooth: [39]But I say unto you, That ye resist not evil: but whosoever shall smite thee on thy right cheek, turn to him the other also.

Adam to the Fall of mankind was not to eat of the tree of the knowledge of good and evil. And Adam to Noah was more of the altar of sacrifice and is what is right in your eyes, because there were no laws at this point. And Noah to Moses same thing.

Moses to Jesus was under the Old Covenant laws. And Jesus to the Rapture and up to the seven-year tribulation is under the grace period.

The seven-year tribulation if one is in that generation and living in the seven years to be saved from the lake of fire It is simply, but will be hard to do, just do not taking the mark and refuse to denounce God or Jesus regardless of how severe the repercussion would be for refusing the mark.

The two nations are like two servants of an owner of a field in a garden getting the last of the harvest to take back to his barn, so the owner can get ready to plan to redo the field, by getting rid of the unwanted weeds, and leftover vines to get the ground back for more and better uses, but it is more like what the scripture said about bundle up the pieces and burn them. And where there will be weeping and gnashing teeth.

Matthew 13:30

> Let both grow together until the harvest: and in the time of harvest I will say to the reapers, Gather ye together first the tares, and bind them in bundles to burn them: but gather the wheat into my barn.

Luke 13:28, "There shall be weeping and gnashing of teeth, when ye shall see Abraham, and Isaac, and Jacob, and all the prophets, in the kingdom of God, and you yourselves thrust out."

2 Peter 3:8, "But, beloved, be not ignorant of this one thing, that one day is with the Lord as a thousand years, and a thousand years as one day."

Psalms 90:4, "For a thousand years in thy sight are but as yesterday when it is past, and as a watch in the night."

With humankind, a day is 24 hours, which can be broken down into hours, minutes, or even seconds.

Humankind is limited and what someone can do in one day some people work eight hours, others may work 12 hours; with this being said, those that work eight hours are limited with 16 hours to accomplish things they want done or need to get done, plus accounting for time that is leftover time that a person has left. The same for the 12-hour workers, except they only have 12 hours left with sleep or rest that has to be included in that time.

God is not limited, but according to Scripture, a day in God's time is one thousand years in human time. Keeping this in mind, where humankind is dealing with hours, minutes, and seconds, God is dealing with years and months when coming to his time, so seven years and the tribulation would be like seconds in his dwelling.

The two olive trees that the Scriptures mention are beside God on each side of his throne at this moment with the thought that it is Israel and United States of America in God's time when they are to be the witness in the first half of the tribulation. It would only have been a few days with God in that time of God's time.

Revelation 11:4, "These are the two olive trees, and the two candlesticks standing before the God of the earth."

John drafted the Book of Revelation of the vision that he was allowed to see. We, the readers of Revelation are able to read and see what John saw that is coming in a generation at an appointed time in the future that will be living out what John saw and what we as the readers of John's writing have read about.

What is amazing to me is how he reveals to his people, his children, or even his servants what is going to happen before it ever happens just like Jesus when he told his disciples to go and fit a donkey that has not been ridden by man and that is when that man comes and asks you why you do this, tell him that the master has need of it.

God's timeline is so awesome that he is all-knowing of the beginning and the end and of all things.

Luke 19:30–31

> [30]Saying, Go ye into the village over against you; in the which at your entering ye shall find a colt tied, whereon yet never man sat loose him, and bring him hither. [31]And if any man ask you, Why do ye loose him? thus shall ye say unto him, Because the Lord hath need of him.

Proverbs 15:3, "The eyes of the Lord are in every place, beholding the evil and the good."

Isaiah 46:10, "Declaring the end from the beginning, and from ancient times the things that are not yet done, saying, My counsel shall stand, and I will do all my pleasure."

God is aware of everything going on earth as well as in heaven. Just like with Sodom and Gomorrah.

Genesis 18:20, "And the Lord said, Because the cry of Sodom and Gomorrah is great, and because their sin is very grievous."

Genesis 11:5, "And the Lord came down to see the city and the tower, which the children of men builded."

God is very much aware of what humankind is doing at all times. God shows it when he tells Joseph and the wise men to go a different way because of the dangers that await them.

Matthew 2:13

> And when they were departed, behold, the angel of the Lord appeared to Joseph in a dream, saying, Arise, and take the

young child and his mother, and flee into Egypt, and be thou there until I bring thee word: for Herod will seek the young child to destroy him.

Matthew 2:12, "And being warned of God in a dream that they should not return to Herod, they departed into their own country another way."

God has seen the beginning and the end. God knows the dead and them that will live forever in the New Jerusalem.

The two nations is to get the last of the believers and give the last warning to humankind and prophesy to them of what is to come if they do not turn to God.

Revelation will be most likely being repeated by the two nations to their audience, which we as believers have read many times over.

The two nations cannot be hurt, harmed, or killed till God allows it. This is in the first three years and a half in the seven-year tribulation, which convinces me in the grace period that God will protect me just the same and all other believers as well, knowing he could keep the two nations safe during their time.

God is using these two witnesses in their time, like those Old Testament prophets, for example these prophets.

Ezekiel 3:17, "Son of man, I have made thee a watchman unto the house of Israel: therefore hear the word at my mouth, and give them warning from me."

Jonah 1:2, "Arise, go to Nineveh, that great city, and cry against it; for their wickedness is come up before me."

There was no grace period before the death of Jesus, because the death of Jesus and the resurrection of Jesus are the beginning of the grace period. And there is no grace period after the resurrection of all born-again believers, both dead in Christ Jesus and alive in Christ Jesus, because this is the end of the grace period when the rapture take place.

1 Thessalonians 5:1–5 ¹But of the times and the seasons, brethren, ye have no need that I write unto you. ²For yourselves know perfectly that the day of the Lord so cometh as a thief in the night. ³For when they shall say, Peace and safety; then sudden destruction cometh upon them, as travail upon a woman with child: and they shall not escape. ⁴But ye, brethren, are not in darkness, that that day should overtake you as a thief. ⁵Ye are all the children of light, and the children of the day: we are not of the night, nor of darkness.

Hebrews 10:24–25

> ²⁴And let us consider one another to provoke unto love and to good works: ²⁵Not forsaking the assembling of ourselves together, as the manner of some is but exhorting one another: and so much the more, as ye see the day approaching.

Acts 1:10–11

> ¹⁰And while they looked stedfastly toward heaven as he went up, behold, two men stood by them in white apparel; ¹¹Which also said, Ye men of Galilee, why stand ye gazing up into heaven? this same Jesus, which is taken up from you into heaven, shall so come in like manner as ye have seen him go into heaven.

1 John 2:28, "And now, little children abide in him; that, when he shall appear, we may have confidence, and not be ashamed before him at his coming."

Matthew 24:42, "Watch therefore: for ye know not what hour your Lord doth come."

Luke 17:34–35

> ³⁴I tell you, in that night there shall be two men in one bed; the one shall be taken, and the other shall be left. ³⁵Two women shall be grinding together; the one shall be taken, and the other left.

Matthew 25:1–13

> ¹Then shall the kingdom of heaven be likened unto ten virgins, which took their lamps, and went forth to meet the bridegroom. ²And five of them were wise, and five were foolish. ³They that were foolish took their lamps, and took no oil with them: ⁴But the wise took oil in their vessels with their lamps. ⁵While the bridegroom tarried, they all slumbered and slept. ⁶And at midnight there was a cry made, Behold, the bridegroom cometh; go ye out to meet him. ⁷Then all those virgins arose, and trimmed their lamps. ⁸And the foolish said unto the wise, Give us of your oil; for our lamps are gone out. ⁹But the wise answered, saying, Not so; lest there be not enough for us and you: but go ye rather to them that sell, and buy for yourselves. ¹⁰And while they went to buy, the bridegroom came; and they that were ready went in with him to the marriage: and the door was shut. ¹¹Afterward came also the other virgins, saying, Lord, Lord, open to us. ¹²But he answered and said, Verily I say unto you, I know you not. ¹³Watch therefore, for ye know neither the day nor the hour wherein the Son of man cometh.

When I listen to what Matthew 25:1–13 is saying, "The bridegroom cometh," the verses are not just referring to the Rapture, but that we are the bride of Christ Jesus. And this is the reason for the grace period. Christ's body, New Jerusalem, the bride of Christ, and the Rapture are one in the same.

In the grace period, I as an individual do not work for salvation, but by faith believe the work has been done by God, and all I have to do is receive it as a gift from God.

Ephesians 2:8–9, "⁸For by grace are ye saved through faith; and that not of yourselves: it is the gift of God: ⁹Not of works, lest any man should boast."

Romans 1:17, "For therein is the righteousness of God revealed from faith to faith: as it is written, The just shall live by faith."

Knowing this I have to understand that faith comes by hearing the Word of God.

Romans 10:17, "So then faith cometh by hearing, and hearing by the word of God."

In other words when I hear John 3:16, "For God so loved the world, that he gave his only begotten Son, that whosoever believeth in him should not perish, but have everlasting life," by faith I believe these words and start acting on them. By checking out other scriptures like Romans 10:9–13:

> [9]That if thou shalt confess with thy mouth the Lord Jesus, and shalt believe in thine heart that God hath raised him from the dead, thou shalt be saved. [10]For with the heart man believeth unto righteousness; and with the mouth confession is made unto salvation. [11]For the scripture saith, Whosoever believeth on him shall not be ashamed. [12]For there is no difference between the Jew and the Greek: for the same Lord over all is rich unto all that call upon him. [13]For whosoever shall call upon the name of the Lord shall be saved.

I start a spiritual growth, and my faith as a grain of mustard seed is able to start moving mountains in my life. I achieve things that I did not think were possible such as habits, character, morals, and doing right in the sight of God.

Matthew 17:20

> And Jesus said unto them, Because of your unbelief: for verily I say unto you, If ye have faith as a grain of mustard seed, ye shall say unto this mountain, Remove hence to yonder place; and it shall remove; and nothing shall be impossible unto you.

The more I hear the words, the more my faith grows, and the more I walk by faith, the more my faith is real. It is not blind faith; the more I seek, the more I find and is revealed to me. The more the spirit of God shows me, the more I cannot unsee and I am convinced of the spiritual world or unseen world that can only be seen by faith through grace.

The grace period is very important because God has done all the work, and all I have to do is receive it. And by believing, I start letting God do the work on me that he is able to finish with me from now or until the time of my funeral or the Rapture; either way I have to be ready.

Philippians 1:6, "Being confident of this very thing, that he which hath begun a good work in you will perform it until the day of Jesus Christ."

When I compare the period before grace and the period after grace, they both have something in common and is the opposite of the grace period.

Humankind has to work for salvation before and after the grace period, but not in the grace period.

The two nations come after the grace period. And the start of the seven-year tribulation has started. The one-world order is seizing power and taking control over all governments around the world.

These two nations will have these powers according to Revelation 11:3: "And I will give power unto my two witnesses, and they shall prophesy a thousand two hundred and threescore days, clothed in sackcloth."

The days of salvation as born-again believers know it in the grace period are over. During these three and half years is the taking over by the new-world order or the Antichrist's reign is causing chaos.

The two witnesses which is the two nations will be given their testimonies and will finish their testimonies before they are allowed to be killed. What testimony they will have, I can only imagine.

God called and created these two nations, and these two nations are truly the last witness to the world and the world last chance to be saved from a eternal hell of torment

Revelation 11:4, "These are the two olive trees, and the two candlesticks standing before the God of the earth."

They are not there to preach Jesus the way born-again believers know to do in the grace period. They are there to warn and prophecy the doom and destruction coming on earth and after their death.

There was no more save by grace through faith during the seven-year tribulation; this type of salvation ended when the Rapture took place.

During the grace period, an individual could simply believe God did all the work needed for salvation through the sacrifice of his Son Jesus who was homeless, beaten to unrecognizable, tortured, mocked at, thirsty, hungry, and killed for the wages of my sins and the world's sins. All I have to do is believe it because God has done everything for me and others as well; that way it is not by work that I am saved but by grace through faith, but I also understand the difference in believing and believing there are two types, which is spoken in James 2:16–20:

> [16]And one of you say unto them, Depart in peace, be ye warmed and filled; notwithstanding ye give them not those things which are needful to the body; what doth it profit? [17]Even so faith, if it hath not works, is dead, being alone. [18]Yea, a man may say, Thou hast faith, and I have works: shew me thy faith without thy works, and I will shew thee my faith by my works. [19]Thou believest that there is one God; thou doest well: the devils also believe, and tremble. [20]But wilt thou know, O vain man, that faith without works is dead?

Then there is this in James 2:19: "Thou believest that there is one God; thou doest well: the devils also believe, and tremble."

The difference is real belief has action behind it. Even though it is not my works that saved me, but faith in Jesus alone does. This will cause me to produce work like James said, I see a need, or to do something righteous, I will do it because I believe.

The other belief is like what James said about the demons: they believe the one God and tremble, but they are at war with and work against God.

Another example is the rich man and Lazarus; let us say the rich man believes in one God but did not put the action behind his belief when he refuses to acknowledge Lazarus's needs. This is faith without works.

Luke 16:19–23

> [19]There was a certain rich man, which was clothed in purple and fine linen, and fared sumptuously every day: [20]And there was a certain beggar named Lazarus, which was laid at his gate, full of sores, [21]And desiring to be fed with the crumbs which fell from the rich man's table: moreover the dogs came and licked his sores. [22]And it came to pass, that the beggar died, and was carried by the angels into Abraham's bosom: the rich man also died, and was buried; [23]And in hell he lift up his eyes, being in torments, and seeth Abraham afar off, and Lazarus in his bosom.

Then there was the story of the Good Samaritan; this is an example of the right kind of belief and how to put action behind belief. The Good Samaritan sees an individual that has come upon hard times. Thieves have robbed him, beat him, and left him for dead, but the Good Samaritan not only acknowledges his needs. He acts on it and cleans him up, takes him in town, pays for all his medical and lodging expenses and whatever else is needed for this man, and went as far as to say to the keeper that if he owes anything else when he comes back, he will pay what is owed. This is belief with action, this is work that is produced by faith, and the more faith that I have, the more work I am able to do, but knowing work did not save me, but simply believing in Jesus Christ did, and that is why in the grace period it is said that we do not work for salvation.

Luke 10:33–37

> [33]But a certain Samaritan, as he journeyed, came where he was: and when he saw him, he had compassion on him, [34]And went to him, and bound up his wounds, pouring in oil and wine, and set him on his own beast, and brought him to an inn, and took care of him. [35]And on the morrow when he departed, he took out two pence, and gave them to the

host, and said unto him, Take care of him; and whatsoever thou spendest more, when I come again, I will repay thee. [36]Which now of these three, thinkest thou, was neighbour unto him that fell among the thieves? [37]And he said, He that shewed mercy on him. Then said Jesus unto him, Go, and do thou likewise.

The seven-year tribulation is the opposite of the grace period; now that generation will work for salvation. During the grace period, Jesus suffered for all those generations up to the Rapture, but now those in the tribulation will suffer for Jesus to gain eternal life with Jesus.

Revelation 7:9–17

[9]After this I beheld, and, lo, a great multitude, which no man could number, of all nations, and kindreds, and people, and tongues, stood before the throne, and before the Lamb, clothed with white robes, and palms in their hands; [10]And cried with a loud voice, saying, Salvation to our God which sitteth upon the throne, and unto the Lamb. [11]And all the angels stood round about the throne, and about the elders and the four beasts, and fell before the throne on their faces, and worshipped God, [12]Saying, Amen: Blessing, and glory, and wisdom, and thanksgiving, and honour, and power, and might, be unto our God for ever and ever. Amen. [13]And one of the elders answered, saying unto me, What are these which are arrayed in white robes? and whence came they? [14]And I said unto him, Sir, thou knowest. And he said to me, These are they which came out of great tribulation, and have washed their robes, and made them white in the blood of the Lamb. [15]Therefore are they before the throne of God, and serve him day and night in his temple: and he that sitteth on the throne shall dwell among them. [16]They shall hunger no more, neither thirst anymore; neither shall the sun light on them, nor any heat. [17]For the Lamb which is in the midst of the throne shall feed them, and shall lead them unto living fountains of waters: and God shall wipe away all tears from their eyes.

These scriptures are talking about those in the tribulation that will be saved because they did not take the mark of the beast. They are working for salvation by refusing the mark; they are giving up all rights to being a legal citizen anywhere on earth, but gaining citizenship with Jesus.

Jesus suffered to give me and others a grace period. They are going to suffer as Jesus did to bring the grace period in this present time, and now they have no home, cannot buy or sell, and they have to get by as best they can. And they will die or be jailed for not taking the mark of the beast.

Revelation 13:16–17

> [16]And he causeth all, both small and great, rich and poor, free and bond, to receive a mark in their right hand, or in their foreheads: [17]And that no man might buy or sell, save he that had the mark, or the name of the beast, or the number of his name.

These are what the five virgins are representing. Those who are not ready when the bridegroom comes, or the Rapture, will have to go through this great tribulation and suffer until their death or pass the seven years when New Jerusalem comes down.

The tribulation reminds me of Shadrach, Meshach, and Abednego, where they were to worship the image that the king had built. They refused and were willing to die before they would sin against God. This is what has to be done during that generation. No matter the cost, refuse the mark.

Daniel 3:16–17 [16]Shadrach, Meshach, and Abednego, answered and said to the king, O Nebuchadnezzar, we are not careful to answer thee in this matter. [17]If it be so, our God whom we serve is able to deliver us from the burning fiery furnace, and he will deliver us out of thine hand, O king.

The same goes for the tribulation generation.

One government, one religion, one currency, and one top leader. This is what comes in that tribulation generation. And this is why the two witnesses are sent there from God to expose them and tell them of their destiny coming soon for all who take the mark of the beast and the beast, the prophet, and the Antichrist.

Revelation 19:20

> And the beast was taken, and with him the false prophet that wrought miracles before him, with which he deceived them that had received the mark of the beast, and them that worshipped his image. These both were cast alive into a lake of fire burning with brimstone.

The two witness tell this over and over, and all involved are gnashing their teeth and trying to kill them but cannot till their mission is done. And these two nation of God will be able to kill them instead by fire from their mouth. Again as I said before is missel coming out of a chamber with fire coming out like a mouth. For three and a half years this is going on to the point where the beast comes out of the pit to declare war on them.

Revelation 11:4–5

> 4These are the two olive trees, and the two candlesticks standing before the God of the earth. 5And if any man will hurt them, fire proceedeth out of their mouth, and devoureth their enemies: and if any man will hurt them, he must in this manner be killed.

Revelation 11:7, "And when they shall have finished their testimony, the beast that ascendeth out of the bottomless pit shall make war against them, and shall overcome them, and kill them."

This war started in heaven but will end on earth. This future event will be very brutal—no more turning the other cheek.

The two last witnesses will be given great power to defend and retaliate against their enemies. There will be innumerable attempts on these two witnesses' lives, and they will return their attempts to their own demise with fire coming out of their mouth to burn them alive and kill them. This is very brutal; there is no more show of mercy.

The grace period has passed by, and now the worst event in history is underway, with these last witnesses prophecy and warning and three and a half years to get as many to refuse the mark of the beast, and this is the only mercy that is given.

That is knowing that this is it, there is no more chances. If one takes the mark, that mark says that the individual has denounced his or her religion, faith, and God. In reality they now belong to the new-world order, which is run by the Antichrist, beast, prophet, and their own religion, which puts him the Antichrist as the god on earth and to be worshipped.

When I look at these two last witnesses, I am reminded of Matthew 20:16: "So the last shall be first, and the first last: for many be called, but few chosen. "These two witnesses being Israel and The United States of America they are last to be rapture will be first. Those of the rapture in the grace period are the first, but will be last. Regardless we all be at the supper table with God.

That is why when they are finally killed and after three and a half days, the Holy Ghost raises them from the dead and are carried back to the supper table with the rest of the family of God and body of Christ.

The dove and olive branch is a picture of this scene with these two witnesses' death and resurrection and being carried back to the Ark.

These two witnesses, while in that generation, are not telling people to go to the church or are preaching in church somewhere, because there is no church for them. The Antichrist's laws in government have taken over all the religions, and there cannot be any other religion other than what the government has created for the world.

I am reminded of Matthew 16:25–27

> 25For whosoever will save his life shall lose it: and whosoever will lose his life for my sake shall find it. 26For what is a man profited, if he shall gain the whole world, and lose his own soul? or what shall a man give in exchange for his soul? 27For the Son of man shall come in the glory of his Father with

his angels; and then he shall reward every man according to his works.

Those in that generation are given the choice of the mark to live and be free, or not take the mark and die, or lose their freedom.

Just as Jeremiah was the last prophet to preach to the southern kingdom of Israel, so are these last two witness to humankind before their destruction comes.

Just as Jeremiah was called the weeping prophet because of his tender heart, and also knowing what was going to happen to Israel if they did not listen and obey what God has him telling them, so is God by allowing these last two witness to warn humankind one last time.

This really shows God's tenderness and compassion because he does not have to. God already knows the outcome.

Just as Jeremiah was called the weeping prophet, so is God when it comes to his creation; he did not want to destroy humankind in Noah's days. And he does not want to destroy humankind in that time. Jesus is the very image of God. And what does he say to his father as they are killing him on the cross?

Luke 23:34, "Then said Jesus, Father, forgive them; for they know not what they do. And they parted his raiment, and cast lots."

God knows this to be even so in the tribulation generation, so he allow the two witnesses to prophecy; this is the last chance for any human in that generation to escape what is coming on earth and what is waiting on the other side when their life has left This is even so in my generation or the generations to come before the tribulation. Because they are on one of two locations after they die. And the choice I make while I am alive determines which location I will go when I die.

Luke 16:22–23

> [22]And it came to pass, that the beggar died, and was carried by the angels into Abraham's bosom: the rich man also died, and was buried; [23]And in hell he lift up his eyes, being in

torments, and seeth Abraham afar off, and Lazarus in his bosom. This is the best way to acknowledge this.

There is no do-over when I leave this prison of my body as Dotty Rambo's song said. There is no coming back to do it over. I got all the chances while I am alive, but when dead, it is final. Listen what Abraham tells the rich man.

Luke 16:27–31

> [27]Then he said, I pray thee therefore, father, that thou wouldest send him to my father's house: [28]For I have five brethren; that he may testify unto them, lest they also come into this place of torment. [29]Abraham saith unto him, They have Moses and the prophets; let them hear them. [30]And he said, Nay, Father Abraham: but if one went unto them from the dead, they will repent. [31]And he said unto him, If they hear not Moses and the prophets, neither will they be persuaded, though one rose from the dead.

I know one did raise from the grave, and his name is Jesus Christ, God with man, Son of God, the Lamb that takes away the sins of the world, and the only way to salvation and God.

Since the Fall of humankind he has made a way for humankind to return to him, and his name is Jesus.

John 11:25–26, "[25]Jesus said unto her, I am the resurrection, and the life: he that believeth in me, though he were dead, yet shall he live: [26]And whosoever liveth and believeth in me shall never die. Believest thou this?"

Mark 16:6–7

> [6]And he saith unto them, Be not affrighted: Ye seek Jesus of Nazareth, which was crucified: he is risen; he is not here: behold the place where they laid him. [7]But go your way, tell his disciples and Peter that he goeth before you into Galilee: there shall ye see him, as he said unto you.

Matthew 1:23, "Behold, a virgin shall be with child, and shall bring forth a son, and they shall call his name Emmanuel, which being interpreted is, God with us."

John 1:29, "The next day John seeth Jesus coming unto him, and saith, Behold the Lamb of God, which taketh away the sin of the world."

Luke 1:35 And the angel answered and said unto her, The Holy Ghost shall come upon thee, and the power of the Highest shall overshadow thee: therefore also that holy thing which shall be born of thee shall be called the Son of God.

John 14:6–7

> [6]Jesus saith unto him, I am the way, the truth, and the life: no man cometh unto the Father, but by me. [7]If ye had known me, ye should have known my Father also: and from henceforth ye know him, and have seen him.

When these two witnesses are finally allowed to die and lie in the street for three and a half days before they are resurrected is the picture of what the Lord showed me as the dove carry the olive branch back to the Ark. the Holy Ghost carry these final children of God back to the rest of the family in heaven. And the Holy Ghost and these to witnesses leave earth.

The Holy Ghost leaves as well, and Satan and his kingdom and humankind have the whole earth without God for three and half years.

These two witnesses will truly be the last two witnesses for humankind as the Holy Ghost leaves earth and takes them with him. This is the picture of the dove and the olive branch.

CHAPTER 7

THE DESCENT OF THE ARK

The millennium as revelation tells us in Revelation 20:4:

> And I saw thrones, and they sat upon them, and judgment
> was given unto them: and I saw the souls of them that
> were beheaded for the witness of Jesus, and for the word of
> God, and which had not worshipped the beast, neither his
> image, neither had received his mark upon their foreheads,
> or in their hands; and they lived and reigned with Christ a
> thousand years.

I was confused about the New Jerusalem coming down after reading
Revelation 21:1–2:

> [1]And I saw a new heaven and a new earth: for the first heaven
> and the first earth had passed away; and there was no more
> sea. [2]And I John saw the holy city, new Jerusalem, coming
> down from God out of heaven, prepared as a bride adorned
> for her husband. Then I realize it two different events.

This was important to me because my Father was showing me with his
Spirit that the Ark descending down as the waters started to recede is a
picture of New Jerusalem coming down to reign for a thousand years,
but how is this possible, I thought, when John saw New Jerusalem
coming down. When there are no more people and a new heaven and
earth.

Revelation 20:4 makes it clear that Jesus reigns a thousand years and
then lets Satan out of the bottomless pit for a season.

Revelation 20:3

> And cast him into the bottomless pit, and shut him up, and set a seal upon him, that he should deceive the nations no more, till the thousand years should be fulfilled: and after that he must be loosed a little season. After the thousand years are done.

I realize these are two different events. The first event is where King Jesus comes down to rule for a thousand years with those that have not worshipped the beast and have not taken the mark of the beast in their foreheads or hands, or just simply survive the seven years.

Listen to what Micah said in Micah 4:1–6:

> ¹But in the last days it shall come to pass, that the mountain of the house of the Lord shall be established in the top of the mountains, and it shall be exalted above the hills; and people shall flow unto it. ²And many nations shall come, and say, Come, and let us go up to the mountain of the Lord, and to the house of the God of Jacob; and he will teach us of his ways, and we will walk in his paths: for the law shall go forth of Zion, and the word of the Lord from Jerusalem. ³And he shall judge among many people, and rebuke strong nations afar off; and they shall beat their swords into plowshares, and their spears into pruninghooks: nation shall not lift up a sword against nation, neither shall they learn war anymore. ⁴But they shall sit every man under his vine and under his fig tree; and none shall make them afraid: for the mouth of the Lord of hosts hath spoken it. ⁵For all people will walk everyone in the name of his god, and we will walk in the name of the Lord our God for ever and ever. ⁶In that day, saith the Lord, will I assemble her that halted, and I will gather her that is driven out, and her that I have afflicted; ⁷And I will make her that halted a remnant, and her that was cast far off a strong nation: and the Lord shall reign over them in mount Zion from henceforth, even for ever.

The thousand-year reign is not the end, or end of days, but is part of the last days.

Micah 4:1, "But in the last days it shall come to pass, that the mountain of the house of the LORD shall be established in the top of the mountains, and it shall be exalted above the hills; and people shall flow unto it."

The thousand years' reign is truly the last days for humankind.

I can only imagine what it would be like during those one thousand years as Jesus reigns over all the nations teaching them.

Micah 4:2

> And many nations shall come, and say, Come, and let us go up to the mountain of the Lord, and to the house of the God of Jacob; and he will teach us of his ways, and we will walk in his paths: for the law shall go forth of Zion, and the word of the Lord from Jerusalem.

Even during that time period, people will still have other gods. Micah 4:5, "For all people will walk everyone in the name of his god, and we will walk in the name of the Lord our God for ever and ever."

Just as the Ark finally was on dry ground, those eight people were the new leaders of the whole world.

The kingdom coming down and sitting on the mountain top is that same picture of the Ark landing.

Jesus and the body of Christ Jesus are the new leaders of the world during this period.

Thinking of my Lord and the kingdom coming down and resting on top of a mountain is awesome because I am reminded of Revelation 22:13, "I am Alpha and Omega, the beginning, and the end, the first and the last."

The Ark rested on top of a mountain; Mount Ararat is to be where the Ark rested, largely because it would have been the first peak to emerge from the receding flood waters. And my Lord Jesus and the kingdom rested on to the top of the mountain, which will be exalted above all hills.

God is over all, all-knowing, all-powerful, all-present, and is the top ruler of heaven and earth. He is able to see past, present, and future at once.

Isaiah 55:11, "So shall my word be that goeth forth out of my mouth: it shall not return unto me void, but it shall accomplish that which I please, and it shall prosper in the thing whereto I sent it."

Psalms 147:5, "Great is our Lord, and of great power: his understanding is infinite."

1 Chronicles 29:11

> Thine, O Lord is the greatness, and the power, and the glory, and the victory, and the majesty: for all that is in the heaven and in the earth is thine; thine is the kingdom, O Lord, and thou art exalted as head above all.

God used the days of Noah from beginning to end and had it recorded in a book so his children would be able to read it in each generation of life, with the help and understanding from the Spirit of God to see the plan of salvation and the end result of all things to come.

When I compare the resting of the Ark and the kingdom of my Lord Jesus, none would have been possible unless the Ark and the kingdom were built.

This is why it so important during the days of Noah to keep working on the Ark because one day Noah and his family would come out of the Ark and be the new leaders of the whole world, just as my Lord and Savior and his kingdom when it comes down to rest on the mountain to be the new leader of the whole world for a thousand years.

To know the truth behind both the Ark and the kingdom is awesome. And how one saved humankind also shows a parallel to the kingdom of God to save the souls of God's children.

This is a reminder that the Ark is a picture of the body of Christ, where he is the chief cornerstone.

Ephesians 2:20–22

> [20]And are built upon the foundation of the apostles and prophets, Jesus Christ himself being the chief corner stone; [21]In whom all the building fitly framed together growth unto an holy temple in the Lord: [22]In whom ye also are builded together for an habitation of God through the Spirit.

1 Corinthians 12:12–27

> [12]For as the body is one, and hath many members, and all the members of that one body, being many, are one body: so also is Christ. [13]For by one Spirit are we all baptized into one body, whether we be Jews or Gentiles, whether we be bond or free; and have been all made to drink into one Spirit. [14]For the body is not one member, but many. [15]If the foot shall say, Because I am not the hand, I am not of the body; is it therefore not of the body? [16]And if the ear shall say, Because I am not the eye, I am not of the body; is it therefore not of the body? [17]If the whole body were an eye, where were the hearing? If the whole were hearing, where were the smelling? [18]But now hath God set the members every one of them in the body, as it hath pleased him. [19]And if they were all one member, where were the body? [20]But now are they many members, yet but one body. [21]And the eye cannot say unto the hand, I have no need of thee: nor again the head to the feet, I have no need of you. [22]Nay, much more those members of the body, which seem to be more feeble, are necessary: [23]And those members of the body, which we think to be less honorable, upon these we bestow more abundant honour; and our uncomely parts have more abundant comeliness. [24]For our comely parts have no need: but God hath tempered the body together, having given more abundant honour to that part which lacked. [25]That there should be no schism in the body; but that the members should have the same care one for another. [26]And

whether one member suffer, all the members suffer with it; or one member be honored, all the members rejoice with it. [27]Now ye are the body of Christ, and members in particular.

This is what I came to understand: both the Ark and the kingdom or New Jerusalem are the same thought when it comes to the body of Christ. And this gives me a clear understanding of both.

The Ark again is just a reminder: it is made of trees that must be cut down and be transformed into whatever is to be used on or the making of the Ark. Not every piece will have the same shape, size, or even purpose.

The children of God are the same thing, and this is what Paul was trying to get the reader to understand. I am like the tree that has to be cut down and transformed into what God has made me for and the purpose and position in the Kingdom as well. This is what it means to die to oneself. The tree cannot become part of the body of the Ark unless it dies, no more than I can become part of the body of Christ if I do not die to self.

It is easy for a tree to die to itself because it gets cut down and someone shapes and cuts it, one might say, which is true.

Noah is a picture of a God-chosen tree, which is me, to cut down or die to self to be used in his body, the kingdom that will come down as already stated like the Ark on the highest mountain.

John 15:16

> Ye have not chosen me, but I have chosen you, and ordained you, that ye should go and bring forth fruit, and that your fruit should remain that whatsoever ye shall ask of the Father in my name, he may give it you.

Philippians 1:6, "Being confident of this very thing, that he which hath begun a good work in you will perform it until the day of Jesus Christ."

Luke 9:23, "And he said to them all, If any man will come after me, let him deny himself, and take up his cross daily, and follow me."

Galatians 2:20–21

> [20]I am crucified with Christ: nevertheless I live; yet not I,
> but Christ liveth in me: and the life which I now live in
> the flesh I live by the faith of the Son of God, who loved
> me, and gave himself for me. [21]I do not frustrate the grace
> of God: for if righteousness come by the law, then Christ is
> dead in vain.

How do I die to myself to be part of this Kingdom, one might ask.

I came to understand as the Word of God became flesh and is Jesus
and dwelt among men. I would have to become the Word of God and
become like Jesus and dwell among men.

Jesus is holy and righteous, and God put him on flesh to die for
humankind's sins to pay for every sin committed past, present, and
future sins. The wages of sin have been paid in full for all humankind.

John 1:14, "And the Word was made flesh, and dwelt among us, (and
we beheld his glory, the glory as of the only begotten of the Father,) full
of grace and truth."

Romans 13:14, "But put ye on the Lord Jesus Christ, and make not
provision for the flesh, to fulfil the lusts thereof."

Galatians 3:27, "For as many of you as have been baptized into Christ
have put on Christ."

Putting on Jesus Christ means putting on the Word of God, becoming
the Word of God. Where Jesus became flesh, I become the Word of
God, reading, studying, and meditating on the Word of God, and
absorbing the Word of God in my mind

2 Timothy 2:15, "Study to shew thyself approved unto God, a workman
that needed not to be ashamed, rightly dividing the word of truth."

Joshua 1:8

> This book of the law shall not depart out of thy mouth; but
> thou shalt meditate therein day and night, that thou mayest

observe to do according to all that is written therein: for then thou shalt make thy way prosperous, and then thou shalt have good success.

Philippians 4:8

> Finally, brethren, whatsoever things are true, whatsoever things are honest, whatsoever things are just, whatsoever things are pure, whatsoever things are lovely, whatsoever things are of good report; if there be any virtue, and if there be any praise, think on these things.

This is what I came to understand about being part of the kingdom of God.

He chose me, he is doing the work on me, and he will be able to finish the work he started to prepare me for the Kingdom.

Noah choosing trees for the Ark is to me a picture of God picking and choosing people for the Kingdom.

Matthew 22:14, "For many are called, but few are chosen."

We know the Word became flesh and that flesh is Jesus. According to John 1:14, "And the Word was made flesh, and dwelt among us, (and we beheld his glory, the glory as of the only begotten of the Father,) full of grace and truth."

Knowing this I wanted to compare the two and see the comparison myself.

Word: Psalms 119:105, "Thy word is a lamp unto my feet, and a light unto my path."

John 8:12, "Then spake Jesus again unto them, saying, I am the light of the world: he that followed me shall not walk in darkness, but shall have the light of life."

Word: Hebrews 4:12

> For the word of God is quick, and powerful, and sharper than any two-edged sword, piercing even to the dividing

asunder of soul and spirit, and of the joints and marrow, and is a discerner of the thoughts and intents of the heart.

Matthew 28:18, "And Jesus came and spake unto them, saying, All power is given unto me in heaven and in earth." John 5:27, "And hath given him authority to execute judgment also, because he is the Son of man." John 1:48, "Nathanael saith unto him, Whence knowest thou me? Jesus answered and said unto him, Before that Philip called thee, when thou was under the fig tree, I saw thee." John 13:26, "Jesus answered, He it is, to whom I shall give a sop, when I have dipped it. And when he had dipped the sop, he gave it to Judas Iscariot, the son of Simon." John 2:24, "But Jesus did not commit himself unto them, because he knew all men." John 2:25, "And needed not that any should testify of man: for he knew what was in man." John 11:44, "And he that was dead came forth, bound hand and foot with graveclothes: and his face was bound about with a napkin. Jesus saith unto them, Loose him, and let him go." John 18:6, "As soon then as he had said unto them, I am him, they went backward, and fell to the ground." Matthew 26:53, "Thinkest thou that I cannot now pray to my Father, and he shall presently give me more than twelve legions of angels?"

The Word put on flesh, who is righteous, holy, perfect, and God to become man, who is sinful, unrighteous, evil, and not perfect, to die for humankind, so they could die to self or flesh to become the Word or Jesus.

Jesus said this at 12 years old: Luke 2:49, "And he said unto them, How is it that ye sought me? wist ye not that I must be about my Father's business?"

This was true before and is true today—the building of the kingdom of God, with him being the king of the Kingdom.

King Jesus is a king of a Kingdom that will never end—the eternal government of heaven and earth.

The New Jerusalem coming down is a picture that Noah is showing, from God's design from Noah's life as he descended with the water to dry ground on top of a mountain.

Just as Noah is the leader of the new world or earth, so will Jesus be when New Jerusalem comes down with his kingdom to set on a high mountain to be the leader of earth for a thousand years.

Jesus's kingship, I was shown through the word with my Heavenly Father's help. This is what I learned.

1 Kings 1:33–34

> [33]The king also said unto them, Take with you the servants of your lord, and cause Solomon my son to ride upon mine own mule, and bring him down to Gihon: [34]And let Zadok the priest and Nathan the prophet anoint him there king over Israel: and blow ye with the trumpet, and say, God save king Solomon.

Mark 11:7–11

> [7]And they brought the colt to Jesus, and cast their garments on him; and he sat upon him. [8]And many spread their garments in the way: and others cut down branches off the trees, and strawed them in the way. [9]And they that went before, and they that followed, cried, saying, Hosanna; Blessed is he that cometh in the name of the Lord: [10]Blessed be the kingdom of our father David, that cometh in the name of the Lord: Hosanna in the highest. [11]And Jesus entered into Jerusalem, and into the temple: and when he had looked round about upon all things, and now the eventide was come, he went out unto Bethany with the twelve.

Our Heavenly Father was showing the religious crowd and the readers of his Word when it comes to publish that he had proclaimed Jesus king. Even the religious crowd knew this, and king he is, but not the way they thought.

Even Jesus said he was a king when he declared this to Pilate.

John 18:33–37

> [33]Then Pilate entered into the judgment hall again, and called Jesus, and said unto him, Art thou the King of the Jews? [34]Jesus answered him, Sayest thou this thing of thyself, or did others tell it thee of me? [35]Pilate answered, Am I a Jew? Thine own nation and the chief priests have delivered thee unto me: what hast thou done? [36]Jesus answered, My kingdom is not of this world: if my kingdom were of this world, then would my servants fight, that I should not be delivered to the Jews: but now is my kingdom not from hence. [37]Pilate therefore said unto him, Art thou a king then? Jesus answered, Thou sayest that I am a king. To this end was I born, and for this cause came I into the world, that I should bear witness unto the truth. Everyone that is of the truth heareth my voice. Jesus was saying yes am a king, but not of this world. without saying am a king, but also told Pilate he does have a kingdom.

When Jesus said this; John 15:18–20

> [18]If the world hate you, ye know that it hated me before it hated you. [19]If ye were of the world, the world would love his own: but because ye are not of the world, but I have chosen you out of the world, therefore the world hatest you. [20]Remember the word that I said unto you, The servant is not greater than his lord. If they have persecuted me, they will also persecute you; if they have kept my saying, they will keep yours also.

The same Jesus told Pilate that his kingdom is not of this world is saying something to his believer: that we, the born-again believers, are not of this world, but of the world or kingdom coming, New Jerusalem, where Jesus is king and the born-again are citizens.

The world hates the master, and the master said the world would hate the born-again believer; who are the world Jesus speaks of?

The world are those leaders with great influence such as government officials and religious leaders that can influence others or even deceive others and manipulate others.

Jesus is coming into Jerusalem being praised.

John 12:12–15

> 12On the next day much people that were come to the feast, when they heard that Jesus was coming to Jerusalem, 13Took branches of palm trees, and went forth to meet him, and cried, Hosanna: Blessed is the King of Israel that cometh in the name of the Lord. 14And Jesus, when he had found a young ass, sat thereon; as it is written, 15Fear not, daughter of Sion: behold, thy King cometh, sitting on an ass's colt.

Jesus hearing the same people yelling crucify him, crucify him.

Luke 23:21–23

> 21But they cried, saying, Crucify him, crucify him. 22And he said unto them the third time, Why, what evil hath he done? I have found no cause of death in him: I will therefore chastise him, and let him go. 23And they were instant with loud voices, requiring that he might be crucified. And the voices of them and of the chief priests prevailed.

What happens is the people stopped thinking for themselves and started to listen to the corrupt chief priests, because even Pilate said, I do not see anything worthy of death.

This had to be done, and Jesus knew his father was allowing this for the better good of human souls, but it did not excuse them just because this event was all according to God's plan.

John 19:11, "Jesus answered, Thou couldest have no power at all against me, except it were given thee from above: therefore he that delivered me unto thee hath the greater sin."

Pilate was not without sin, but the chief priests' sin was the greater sin; Pilate could have released him, because of his authority, but Jesus knew his father put him there to carry out the greatest gift for humankind.

The real enemy is not flesh and blood, nor governments. As a matter of fact we are told to obey those in authority over us and in this scripture:

Romans 13:1–7

> [1]Let every soul be subject unto the higher powers. For there is no power but of God: the powers that be are ordained of God. [2]Whosoever therefore resisted the power, resisted the ordinance of God: and they that resist shall receive to themselves damnation. [3]For rulers are not a terror to good works, but to the evil. Wilt thou then not be afraid of the power? do that which is good, and thou shalt have praise of the same: [4]For he is the minister of God to thee for good. But if thou do that which is evil, be afraid; for he beareth not the sword in vain: for he is the minister of God, a revenger to execute wrath upon him that doeth evil. [5]Wherefore ye must needs be subject, not only for wrath, but also for conscience sake. [6]For for this cause pay ye tribute also: for they are God's ministers, attending continually upon this very thing. [7]Render therefore to all their dues: tribute to whom tribute is due; custom to whom custom; fear to whom fear; honour to whom honour.

I looked at several incidents in the scripture that show just that. They obeyed authority above them, unto their death sentence, but did not die

Daniel 3:15–17

> [15]Now if ye be ready that at what time ye hear the sound of the cornet, flute, harp, sackbut, psaltery, and dulcimer, and all kinds of music, ye fall down and worship the image which I have made; well: but if ye worship not, ye shall be cast the same hour into the midst of a burning fiery furnace; and who is that God that shall deliver you out of my hands? [16]Shadrach, Meshach, and Abednego, answered and said to the king, O Nebuchadnezzar, we are not careful to answer

thee in this matter. [17]If it be so, our God whom we serve is able to deliver us from the burning fiery furnace, and he will deliver us out of thine hand, O king.

In this case they were obeying the highest of higher powers, God, but not being hateful or rebellious but accepting the punishment. They were obeying both God by not worshiping the idol and the king by accepting punishment for their choice on the matter.

Daniel 6:1–28

[1]It pleased Darius to set over the kingdom an hundred and twenty princes, which should be over the whole kingdom; [2]And over these three presidents; of whom Daniel was first: that the princes might give accounts unto them, and the king should have no damage. [3]Then this Daniel was preferred above the presidents and princes, because an excellent spirit was in him; and the king thought to set him over the whole realm. [4]Then the presidents and princes sought to find occasion against Daniel concerning the kingdom; but they could find none occasion nor fault; forasmuch as he was faithful, neither was there any error or fault found in him. [5]Then said these men, We shall not find any occasion against this Daniel, except we find it against him concerning the law of his God. [6]Then these presidents and princes assembled together to the king, and said thus unto him, King Darius, live forever. [7]All the presidents of the kingdom, the governors, and the princes, the counsellors, and the captains, have consulted together to establish a royal statute, and to make a firm decree, that whosoever shall ask a petition of any God or man for thirty days, save of thee, O king, he shall be cast into the den of lions. [8]Now, O king, establish the decree, and sign the writing, that it be not changed, according to the law of the Medes and Persians, which altered not. [9]Wherefore king Darius signed the writing and the decree. [10]Now when Daniel knew that the writing was signed, he went into his house; and his windows being open in his chamber toward Jerusalem, he kneeled upon his

knees three times a day, and prayed, and gave thanks before his God, as he did aforetime. [11]Then these men assembled, and found Daniel praying and making supplication before his God. [12]Then they came near, and spoke before the king concerning the king's decree; Hast thou not signed a decree, that every man that shall ask a petition of any God or man within thirty days, save of thee, O king, shall be cast into the den of lions? The king answered and said, The thing is true, according to the law of the Medes and Persians, which altered not. [13]Then answered they and said before the king, That Daniel, which is of the children of the captivity of Judah, regardeth not thee, O king, nor the decree that thou hast signed, but maketh his petition three times a day. [14]Then the king, when he heard these words, was sore displeased with himself, and set his heart on Daniel to deliver him: and he laboured till the going down of the sun to deliver him. [15]Then these men assembled unto the king, and said unto the king, Know, O king, that the law of the Medes and Persians is, That no decree nor statute which the king establisheth may be changed. [16]Then the king commanded, and they brought Daniel, and cast him into the den of lions. Now the king spake and said unto Daniel, Thy God whom thou servest continually, he will deliver thee. [17]And a stone was brought, and laid upon the mouth of the den; and the king sealed it with his own signet, and with the signet of his lords; that the purpose might not be changed concerning Daniel. [18]Then the king went to his palace, and passed the night fasting: neither were instruments of music brought before him: and his sleep went from him. [19]Then the king arose very early in the morning, and went in haste unto the den of lions. [20]And when he came to the den, he cried with a lamentable voice unto Daniel: and the king spake and said to Daniel, O Daniel, servant of the living God, is thy God, whom thou servest continually, able to deliver thee from the lions? [21]Then said Daniel unto the king, O king, live forever. [22]My God hath sent his angel, and hath shut the lions' mouths, that they have not hurt me: forasmuch as before him innocence was found in me; and also before thee, O king, have I done no hurt. ²³Then was the king exceedingly glad for him, and commanded that they should take Daniel up out of the den. So Daniel was taken up out of the den, and no manner of hurt was found upon him, because he believed in his God. ²⁴And the king commanded, and they brought those men which had accused Daniel, and they cast them into the den of lions, them, their children, and their wives; and the lions had the mastery of them, and brake all their bones in pieces or ever they came at the bottom of the den. ²⁵Then king Darius wrote unto all people, nations, and languages, that dwell in all the earth; Peace be multiplied unto you. ²⁶I make a decree, That in every dominion of my kingdom men tremble and fear before the God of Daniel: for he is the living God, and steadfast forever, and his kingdom that which shall not be destroyed, and his dominion shall be even unto the end. ²⁷He delivered and rescue, and he worketh signs and wonders in heaven and in earth, who hath delivered Daniel from the power of the lions. ²⁸So this Daniel prospered in the reign of Darius, and in the reign of Cyrus the Persian.

A child of God is to obey God, and kings, leaders and any authority figures and their laws as long as it does not go against God commandments and laws. Same thing here, obeying authority above us, but God is above all, then human leaders; God is all to be obeyed first in authority and when in difference to man is the only time to not obey, but with every consequence, accept it as a good steward.

Acts 5:29–32

²⁹Then Peter and the other apostles answered and said, We ought to obey God rather than men. ³⁰The God of our fathers raised up Jesus, whom ye slew and hanged on a tree. ³¹Him hath God exalted with his right hand to be a Prince and a Saviour, for to give repentance to Israel, and forgiveness of sins. ³²And we are his witnesses of these things; and so is

also the Holy Ghost, whom God hath given to them that obey him.

Here are the real enemies. Ephesians 6:12, "For we wrestle not against flesh and blood, but against principalities, against powers, against the rulers of the darkness of this world, against spiritual wickedness in high places."

These are the real enemies working behind the scenes of leaders' minds in high places.

Here are some scriptures of spirits working behind the scenes, the very first encounter.

Genesis 3:1–7

> [1]Now the serpent was more subtill than any beast of the field which the Lord God had made. And he said unto the woman, Yea, hath God said, Ye shall not eat of every tree of the garden? [2]And the woman said unto the serpent, We may eat of the fruit of the trees of the garden: [3]But of the fruit of the tree, which is in the midst of the garden, God hath said, Ye shall not eat of it, neither shall ye touch it, lest ye die. [4]And the serpent said unto the woman, Ye shall not surely die: [5]For God doth know that in the day ye eat thereof, then your eyes shall be opened, and ye shall be as gods, knowing good and evil. [6]And when the woman saw that the tree was good for food, and that it was pleasant to the eyes, and a tree to be desired to make one wise, she took of the fruit thereof, and did eat, and gave also unto her husband with her; and he did eat. [7]And the eyes of them both were opened, and they knew that they were naked; and they sewed fig leaves together, and made themselves aprons.

This was not just an attack on humankind, but on God as well. Satan had to get humankind to fall, so he could build his kingdom on this world. He only used Eve to get to Adam, to get his plan to work, which led to another attempt to do the same thing to a man named Job.

Job 2:9, "Then said his wife unto him, Dost thou still retain thine integrity? curse God, and die."

Same method of offence from the father of all lies, but the difference is Job did not fall for it as Adam did. Just as much as he told God he will curse you and die, Satan put it in Job's wife's mind to say. want you just curse God and die.

Job 1:11, "But put forth thine hand now, and touch all that he hath, and he will curse thee to thy face."

John 8:44, "Ye are of your father the devil, and the lusts of your father ye will do. He was a murderer from the beginning, and abode not in the truth, because there is no truth in him. When he speakest a lie, he speakest of his own: for he is a liar, and the father of it."

1 Kings 22:20–23

> [20]And the Lord said, Who shall persuade Ahab, that he may go up and fall at Ramothgilead? And one said on this manner, and another said on that manner. [21]And there came forth a spirit, and stood before the Lord, and said, I will persuade him. [22]And the Lord said unto him, Wherewith? And he said, "I will go forth, and I will be a lying spirit in the mouth of all his prophets. And he said, Thou shalt persuade him, and prevail also: go forth, and do so. [23]Now therefore, behold, the Lord hath put a lying spirit in the mouth of all these thy prophets, and the Lord hath spoken evil concerning thee.

To me this is the best picture of working in the spirit world influencing the flesh world.

Isaiah, when he was talking to a king, was not talking to the king but Satan was influencing that particular team just like when Jesus was talking to Peter, yet he was not talking to Peter but rebuking, the spirit that was trying to influence Peter.

Mark 8:33, "But when he had turned about and looked on his disciples, he rebuked Peter, saying, 'Get thee behind me, Satan: for thou savourest not the things that be of God, but the things that be of men.'"

Jesus knew that Peter was being influenced and rebuked the source.

Isaiah 14:12–17

> [12]How art thou fallen from heaven, O Lucifer, son of the morning! how art thou cut down to the ground, which didst weaken the nations! [13]For thou hast said in thine heart, I will ascend into heaven, I will exalt my throne above the stars of God: I will sit also upon the mount of the congregation, in the sides of the north: [14]I will ascend above the heights of the clouds; I will be like the most High. [15]Yet thou shalt be brought down to hell, to the sides of the pit. [16]They that see thee shall narrowly look upon thee, and consider thee, saying, Is this the man that made the earth to tremble, that did shake kingdoms; [17]That made the world as a wilderness, and destroyed the cities thereof; that opened not the house of his prisoners?

This is what it is all about; whether the king knew or did not know that Isaiah was talking to Satan, Satan was definitely influencing the king.

Just as Satan challenged God on the matter of Job, he also challenged God building his kingdom greater than God's Kingdom, but the difference is that God is creating a kingdom of born-again souls in heaven, while Satan is building his kingdom on earth.

I learned all about who will be the ruler of heaven and earth. Satan is building his kingdom on earth, to battle God. The best picture to understand this is the event that happen when the Hebrew children were slaves to pharaoh and the Egyptian nation.

The Hebrew children were ordered to make bricks, which required a harvesting straw drawing water and getting dirt to mix with it. The Hebrew children were required to gather these things to make the product that the pharaoh needed for what he was building. Pharaoh had slave masters that were under him to supervise and watch over the Hebrew children in their daily chores.

Exodus 1:8–14

> [8]Now there arose up a new king over Egypt, which knew not Joseph. [9]And he said unto his people, Behold, the people of the children of Israel are more and mightier than we: [10]Come on, let us deal wisely with them; lest they multiply, and it come to pass, that, when there falleth out any war, they join also unto our enemies, and fight against us, and so get them up out of the land. [11]Therefore they did set over them taskmasters to afflict them with their burdens. And they built for Pharaoh treasure cities, Pithom and Raamses. [12]But the more they afflicted them, the more they multiplied and grew. And they were grieved because of the children of Israel. [13]And the Egyptians made the children of Israel to serve with rigour: [14]And they made their lives bitter with hard bondage, in morter, and in brick, and in all manner of service in the field: all their service, wherein they made them serve, was with rigour.

This is truly a picture of Satan building a kingdom on earth: Satan as Pharaoh, taskmaster as Satan's fallen angels, Hebrew children as humankind, as well as the born-again children of God and Moses as the Lord Jesus.

This is twofold concerning the Hebrew children: first humankind as Satan uses humankind to build his kingdom, which is being done as I write this page.

Humankind may or may not know what they are doing, but they are building Satan's army and his weapons to fight against God at the appointed time by God, which will be AI, robots, that one will not be able to tell the difference between real humans or a AI or robot humans, which will be inhabited with Satan's demon spirit. This is Satan's way of imitating God's version of making life: body, soul, and mind. This is the picture of humankind enslaved by Satan, their father. And Moses represent Jesus, who was sent by God to free humankind from his hold and set them free.

John 8:44

> Ye are of your father the devil, and the lusts of your father ye will do. He was a murderer from the beginning, and abode not in the truth, because there is no truth in him. When he speaketh a lie, he speaketh of his own: for he is a liar, and the father of it.

Till I accepted Jesus and acknowledged that I am a sinner and believe Jesus paid my sins with his life, Satan was my father, but by me accepting Jesus died for my sins and believing it and confessing that I am a sinner, God becomes my father.

John 8:36, "If the Son therefore shall make you free, ye shall be free indeed."

Acts 16:30–31, [30]"And brought them out, and said, Sirs, what must I do to be saved? [31]And they said, Believe on the Lord Jesus Christ, and thou shalt be saved, and thy house."

Second, the Hebrew children are a picture of the born-again being delivered as well. While Satan build his kingdom on earth, with humankind's help, the children of God will escape to the Promised Land.

When New Jerusalem comes down and rests on top the tallest mountain, this represents King Jesus and his body the born-again believers.

One reason I think the city will land on top of the tallest mountain is the fact that Satan said this in his heart: Isaiah 14:13, "For thou hast said in thine heart, I will ascend into heaven, I will exalt my throne above the stars of God: I will sit also upon the mount of the congregation, in the sides of the north."

Man wants to go in outer space, but really Satan is using man to do this but wants to be able to. And Satan will not be able to build his kingdom on earth or the highest point. Satan will never ascend above God.

After the destruction of Satan and humankind's undoing on earth with the wrath of God unleashed on this planet, the new heaven and earth will start, and life will start again as God intended it to be. And the wheat and tare will have been separated from each other for ever.

Revelation 16:1–8

[1]And I heard a great voice out of the temple saying to the seven angels, Go your ways, and pour out the vials of the wrath of God upon the earth. [2]And the first went, and poured out his vial upon the earth; and there fell a noisome and grievous sore upon the men which had the mark of the beast, and upon them which worshipped his image. [3]And the second angel poured out his vial upon the sea; and it became as the blood of a dead man: and every living soul died in the sea. [4]And the third angel poured out his vial upon the rivers and fountains of waters; and they became blood. [5]And I heard the angel of the waters say, Thou art righteous, O Lord, which art, and wast, and shalt be, because thou hast judged thus. [6]For they have shed the blood of saints and prophets, and thou hast given them blood to drink; for they are worthy. [7]And I heard another out of the altar say, Even so, Lord God Almighty, true and righteous are thy judgments. [8]And the fourth angel poured out his vial upon the sun; and power was given unto him to scorch men with fire. [9]And men were scorched with great heat, and blasphemed the name of God, which hath power over these plagues: and they repented not to give him glory. [10]And the fifth angel poured out his vial upon the seat of the beast; and his kingdom was full of darkness; and they gnawed their tongues for pain, [11]And blasphemed the God of heaven because of their pains and their sores, and repented not of their deeds. [12]And the sixth angel poured out his vial upon the great river Euphrates; and the water thereof was dried up, that the way of the kings of the east might be prepared. [13]And I saw three unclean spirits like frogs come out of the mouth of the dragon, and out of the mouth of the beast, and out of the mouth of the false prophet. [14]For they are the

spirits of devils, working miracles, which go forth unto the kings of the earth and of the whole world, to gather them to the battle of that great day of God Almighty. [15]Behold, I come as a thief. Blessed is he that watcheth, and keepeth his garments, lest he walk naked, and they see his shame. [16]And he gathered them together into a place called in the Hebrew tongue Armageddon. [17]And the seventh angel poured out his vial into the air; and there came a great voice out of the temple of heaven, from the throne, saying, It is done. [18]And there were voices, and thunders, and lightnings; and there was a great earthquake, such as was not since men were upon the earth, so mighty an earthquake, and so great. [19]And the great city was divided into three parts, and the cities of the nation's fell: and great Babylon came in remembrance before God, to give unto her the cup of the wine of the fierceness of his wrath. [20]And every island fled away, and the mountains were not found. [21]And there fell upon men a great hail out of heaven, every stone about the weight of a talent: and men blasphemed God because of the plague of the hail; for the plague thereof was exceeding great.

This is just a taste of the wrath of God. And when these events are done, then comes the greatest event the world has ever witnessed: the great Kingdom of God coming down from heaven with the King of kings and Lords of lords. Our Lord God Jesus Christ, our king with his chosen ones to rule and govern the world for a thousand years.

Revelation 20:6–7

[6]Blessed and holy is he that hath part in the first resurrection: on such the second death hath no power, but they shall be priests of God and of Christ, and shall reign with him a thousand years. [7]And when the thousand years are expired, Satan shall be loosed out of his prison,

These are the ones who were resurrected at the beginning of the tribulation to be part of the Kingdom coming.

Revelation 3:12

> Him that overcomes will I make a pillar in the temple of
> my God, and he shall go no more out: and I will write upon
> him the name of my God, and the name of the city of my
> God, which is new Jerusalem, which cometh down out of
> heaven from my God: and I will write upon him my new
> name.

Revelation 21:2, "And I John saw the holy city, new Jerusalem, coming
down from God out of heaven, prepared as a bride adorned for her
husband."

Revelation 19:7–9

> [7]Let us be glad and rejoice, and give honour to him: for
> the marriage of the Lamb is come, and his wife hath made
> herself ready. [8]And to her was granted that she should be
> arrayed in fine linen, clean and white: for the fine linen is
> the righteousness of saints. [9]And he saith unto me, Write,
> Blessed are they who are called unto the marriage supper of
> the Lamb. And he saith unto me, These are the true sayings
> of God.

What a day that will be when the Lord face I shall see. I cannot help but
close this chapter with this.

John 19:19, "And Pilate wrote a title, and put it on the cross. And the
writing was Jesus of Nazareth the King of the Jews."

CHAPTER 8

BOW IN THE CLOUDS

Genesis 9:13–17

> ¹³I do set my bow in the cloud, and it shall be for a token of a covenant between me and the earth. ¹⁴And it shall come to pass, when I bring a cloud over the earth, that the bow shall be seen in the cloud: ¹⁵And I will remember my covenant, which is between me and you and every living creature of all flesh; and the waters shall no more become a flood to destroy all flesh. ¹⁶And the bow shall be in the cloud; and I will look upon it, that I may remember the everlasting covenant between God and every living creature of all flesh that is upon the earth. ¹⁷And God said unto Noah, This is the token of the covenant, which I have established between me and all flesh that is upon the earth.

God had destroyed all flesh and all living things on dry land. He did this to preserve the bloodline of Jesus Christ, which would lead to Mary, Jesus's mother; with this being said, he no longer had to destroy humankind again or all flesh, so he makes this promise with this covenant. Noah and all living creatures on the earth to put this bow or rainbow in the sky, so whenever it rained, or cloud came the rainbow would come forth for God to look upon and remember the covenant in which he promised Noah and all living creatures and all living flesh on the earth to never destroy earth again by water.

God said this in Genesis 9:16, "And the bow shall be in the cloud; and I will look upon it, that I may remember the everlasting covenant between God and every living creature of all flesh that is upon the earth."

Two words stood out to me, "look" and "remember" because God would. The first word, "look," tells me that God is really going to look at that bow. The second word, "remember," tells me that when he looks at it, it will remind him. So what was it that God saw when he looked on the rainbow, because when God does something, I have come to understand there is more to it than meets the eye, more than God just seeing the bow and saying, well I am not going to destroy the earth by water today; I have seen bow. I honestly believe that when he looked at that bow, that rainbow, he saw a lot. And I just want to break it down and see by scripture what God is seeing in that bow.

When God look at this rainbow, he reminded he created this bow. Genesis 1:1, "In the beginning God created the heaven and the earth."

He is also reminded that it takes light and water to bring forth the bow wonderful colors that represent a promise to humankind from God.

God is the light and the water that create the bow and promise

A rainbow can form when both sunshine and water droplets are in the sky. Sunlight is a white light, which is a mixture of all visible colors. As sunlight passes through the water droplets, it is bent and split into seven colors: red, orange, yellow, green, blue, indigo, and violet.

Genesis 1:3–4, "³And God said, Let there be light: and there was light. ⁴And God saw the light, that it was good: and God divided the light from the darkness."

The very first thing he created after heaven and earth was light. This is not sunlight because the sun was created later.

Genesis 1:2–5

> ²And the earth was without form, and void; and darkness was upon the face of the deep. And the Spirit of God moved upon the face of the waters. ³And God said, Let there be light: and there was light. ⁴And God saw the light, that it was good: and God divided the light from the darkness. ⁵And God called the light Day, and the darkness he called Night. And the evening and the morning were the first day.

Genesis 1:14–19

> [14]And God said, Let there be lights in the firmament of the heaven to divide the day from the night; and let them be for signs, and for seasons, and for days, and years: [15]And let them be for lights in the firmament of the heaven to give light upon the earth: and it was so. [16]And God made two great lights; the greater light to rule the day, and the lesser light to rule the night: he made the stars also. [17]And God set them in the firmament of the heaven to give light upon the earth, [18]And to rule over the day and over the night, and to divide the light from the darkness: and God saw that it was good. [19]And the evening and the morning were the fourth day.

He created light first and then three days later created the greater light, the sun.

When God thinks of this, he is reminded of what the light is: his Word. The Word of God is the light.

Psalms 119:105, "Thy word is a lamp unto my feet, and a light unto my path."

Psalms 119:130, "The entrance of thy words giveth light; it giveth understanding unto the simple."

He also sees his Son Jesus as the light to fulfil his promise to Satan in the Garden of Eden.

Genesis 3:14–15

> [14]And the Lord God said unto the serpent, Because thou hast done this, thou art cursed above all cattle, and above every beast of the field; upon thy belly shalt thou go, and dust shalt thou eat all the days of thy life: [15]And I will put enmity between thee and the woman, and between thy seed and her seed; it shall bruise thy head, and thou shalt bruise his heel.

When God looked at the rainbow, he saw his Son Jesus being able to show his promises to the world that would receive him.

John 1:12, "But as many as received him, to them gave he power to become the sons of God, even to them that believe on his name."

John 8:12, "Then spake Jesus again unto them, saying, I am the light of the world: he that followed me shall not walk in darkness, but shall have the light of life."

John 1:14, "And the Word was made flesh, and dwelt among us, (and we beheld his glory, the glory as of the only begotten of the Father,) full of grace and truth."

John 1:8–9, [8]"He was not that Light, but was sent to bear witness of that Light. [9]That was the true Light, which lighted every man that cometh into the world."

The water needed also to make the rainbow is a picture of the Holy Ghost.

Just as much as light and water are needed to make the rainbow, to see the colors in the rainbow, so is the Word of God and the Holy Ghost to see the promises of God.

The light is a picture of the word and Jesus who is the Word of God. The water droplets are a picture of the Holy Ghost that will dwell in God's children to be able to see these promises. The colors are the picture of the promises of God.

John 7:37–39

> [37]In the last day, that great day of the feast, Jesus stood and cried, saying, If any man thirst, let him come unto me, and drink. [38]He that believeth on me, as the scripture hath said, out of his belly shall flow rivers of living water. [39](But this spake he of the Spirit, which they that believe on him should receive: for the Holy Ghost was not yet given; because that Jesus was not yet glorified.)

Isaiah 44:3, "For I will pour water upon him that is thirsty, and floods upon the dry ground: I will pour my spirit upon thy seed, and my blessing upon thine offspring."

John 4:14, "But whosoever drinketh of the water that I shall give him shall never thirst; but the water that I shall give him shall be in him a well of water springing up into everlasting life."

1 Corinthians 12:13, "For by one Spirit are we all baptized into one body, whether we be Jews or Gentiles, whether we be bond or free; and have been all made to drink into one Spirit."

John 4:10, "Jesus answered and said unto her, If thou knewest the gift of God, and who it is that saith to thee, Give me to drink; thou wouldest have asked of him, and he would have given thee living water."

John 4:13–14

> [13]Jesus answered and said unto her, Whosoever drinketh of this water shall thirst again: [14]But whosoever drinketh of the water that I shall give him shall never thirst; but the water that I shall give him shall be in him a well of water springing up into everlasting life.

He sees this bow in the sky and is reminded that the Word of God will be made flesh, and the Holy Ghost will be able to fulfill the promises that were coming; that is why he was able to say this.

Matthew 13:29–30

> [29]But he said, Nay; lest while ye gather up the tares, ye root up also the wheat with them. [30]Let both grow together until the harvest: and in the time of harvest I will say to the reapers, Gather ye together first the tares, and bind them in bundles to burn them: but gather the wheat into my barn.

Even in this he can see the Godhead, Father, Son, and Holy Ghost; just in the making of the bow he sees the trinity that created the bow.

With the Father speaking the word "light," the light being the word, and the Holy Ghost acting on the light to cause the promises to be seen, it is no wonder that God could say this in Genesis 1:31, "And God saw everything that he had made, and behold, it was very good. And the evening and the morning were the sixth day."

There are three primary colors: red, yellow, and blue that make up the other colors, so they can exist.

Red is first, and there a reason for it being first and why God planned it that way, because it reminds him of his Son, Jesus, who would give his life and blood to save the souls of man and pay the debt humankind owed.

When he sees the bow and looks at the first color red and is reminded not to destroy humankind by water again, because his son would pay the sins of all humankind once and for all. With his blood and his body this to is a promise, and it was achieved. That is the reason Jesus said this in Matthew 26:26–27:

> [26]And as they were eating, Jesus took bread, and blessed it, and brake it, and gave it to the disciples, and said, Take, eat; this is my body. [27]And he took the cup, and gave thanks, and gave it to them, saying, Drink ye all of it; 28 For this is my blood of the new testament, which is shed for many for the remission of sins.

God looking on that color red reminded him of why his son, Jesus, must be a sacrifice, by his own words.

Genesis 3:20–21, [20]"And Adam called his wife's name Eve, because she was the mother of all living. [21]Unto Adam also and to his wife did the Lord God make coats of skins, and clothed them."

He knew to clothe humankind in righteousness it would be the same as him killing those animals to take their skins to clothe Adam's and Eve's nakedness and that he would have to kill Jesus to clothe humankind's souls with his righteousness, to be put back in a new body that is not corrupt.

1 Corinthians 15:42–53

> [42]So also is the resurrection of the dead. It is sown in corruption; it is raised in incorruption: [43]It is sown in dishonor; it is raised in glory: it is sown in weakness; it is raised in power: [44]It is sown a natural body; it is raised a spiritual body. There is a natural body, and there is a spiritual body. [45]And so it is written, The first man Adam was made a living soul; the last Adam was made a quickening spirit. [46]Howbeit that was not first which is spiritual, but that which is natural; and afterward that which is spiritual. [47]The first man is of the earth, earthy; the second man is the Lord from heaven. [48]As is the earthy, such are they also that are earthy: and as is the heavenly, such are they also that are heavenly. [49]And as we have borne the image of the earthy, we shall also bear the image of the heavenly. [50]Now this I say, brethren, that flesh and blood cannot inherit the kingdom of God; neither doth corruption inherit incorruption. [51]Behold, I shew you a mystery; We shall not all sleep, but we shall all be changed, [52]In a moment, in the twinkling of an eye, at the last trump: for the trumpet shall sound, and the dead shall be raised incorruptible, and we shall be changed. [53]For this corruptible must put on incorruption, and this mortal must put on immortality.

He reminded how man's soul is dead and has to be born again and the body when it dies goes back to the dust.

Genesis 3:19, "In the sweat of thy face shalt thou eat bread, till thou return unto the ground; for out of it wast thou taken for dust thou art, and unto dust shalt thou return." God is not concerned about the flesh; it is the soul he wants born again so he can put it in a much better body, a heavenly body. God knows as he is reminded of the color red that none of this can help without giving and sacrificing his son for humankind, the same way Abraham was willing to sacrifice his son. Both God and Abraham were willing to sacrifice their sons, their only sons, for other sins that were owed. The only difference is God went through with it, whereas God provided a ram for Abraham so he could spare his son. This ram is a picture of Jesus replacing humankind for paying for their on sins.

Genesis 22:11–13

> [11]And the angel of the Lord called unto him out of heaven, and said, Abraham, Abraham: and he said, Here am I. [12]And he said, Lay not thine hand upon the lad, neither do thou anything unto him: for now I know that thou fearest God, seeing thou hast not withheld thy son, thine only son from me. [13]And Abraham lifted up his eyes, and looked, and behold behind him a ram caught in a thicket by his horns: and Abraham went and took the ram, and offered him up for a burnt offering in the stead of his son.

Matthew 27:46–51

> [46]And about the ninth hour Jesus cried with a loud voice, saying, Eli, Eli, lama Sabathani? that is to say, My God, my God, why hast thou forsaken me? [47]Some of them that stood there, when they heard that, said, This man calleth for Elias. [48]And straightway one of them ran, and took a spunge, and filled it with vinegar, and put it on a reed, and gave him to drink. [49]The rest said, Let be, let us see whether Elias will come to save him. [50]Jesus, when he had cried again with a loud voice, yielded up the ghost. [51]And, behold, the veil of the temple was rent in twain from the top to the bottom; and the earth did quake, and the rocks rent.

Job made a sacrifice for his children, just in case they had sinned, so his children did not have to do anything but benefit and get eternal life if they died, from what their father did, just as God did for mankind.

Job 1:5

> And it was so, when the days of their feasting were gone about, that Job sent and sanctified them, and rose up early in the morning, and offered burnt offerings according to the number of them all: for Job said, It may be that my sons

have sinned, and cursed God in their hearts. Thus did Job continually.

Titus 3:5–7

> [5]Not by works of righteousness which we have done, but according to his mercy he saved us, by the washing of regeneration, and renewing of the Holy Ghost; [6]Which he shed on us abundantly through Jesus Christ our Saviour; [7]That being justified by his grace, we should be made heirs according to the hope of eternal life.

Ephesians 2:8–10

> [8]For by grace are ye saved through faith; and that not of yourselves: it is the gift of God: [9]Not of works, lest any man should boast. [10]For we are his workmanship, created in Christ Jesus unto good works, which God hath before ordained that we should walk in them.

John the Baptist said it best when he said this in John 1:29: "The next day John seeth Jesus coming unto him, and saith, Behold the Lamb of God, which taketh away the sin of the world." This is what God sees when he sees the first color of the rainbow. And without red, he knows the other colors would not matter. And this is a picture of one of the Godheads, Jesus Christ, Son of God.

John 3:16, "For God so loved the world, that he gave his only begotten Son, that whosoever believeth in him should not perish, but have everlasting life."

When God starts seeing the color yellow of the rainbow, he is reminded of the Holy Spirit and his word. Yellow is a picture of light. Both were with God in the beginning.

Genesis 1:2, "And the earth was without form, and void; and darkness was upon the face of the deep. And the Spirit of God moved upon the face of the waters."

John 1:14–15

> [14]And the Word was made flesh, and dwelt among us, (and we beheld his glory, the glory as of the only begotten of the Father,) full of grace and truth. [15]John bare witness of him, and cried, saying, This was he of whom I spake, He that cometh after me is preferred before me: for he was before me.

God already knows that his Word will go forth and light the path of his children that accept his son to come in their hearts, as well as the Holy Ghost afterward.

God is reminded how you cannot have one without the other. He knew ahead of time when Moses said stand still, see the salvation of the Lord, it was a picture of the son of God being lifted up, the Holy Ghost moving on the waters, and the Word of God.

Exodus 14:13

> And Moses said unto the people, Fear ye not, standstill, and see the salvation of the Lord, which he will shew to you today: for the Egyptians whom ye have seen today, ye shall see them again no more forever.

Exodus 14:16, "But lift thou up thy rod, and stretch out thine hand over the sea, and divide it: and the children of Israel shall go on dry ground through the midst of the sea."

Exodus 14:21, "And Moses stretched out his hand over the sea; and the Lord caused the sea to go back by a strong east wind all that night, and made the sea dry land, and the waters were divided."

The lifting of the rod is a picture of the son of God being lifted up, Jesus Christ. The eastern wind is the picture of the Holy Ghost moving on the water. And the water is a picture of the Word of God.

Neither the New Testament nor the Holy Ghost could come till Jesus was lifted up.

John 16:7–13

> ⁷Nevertheless I tell you the truth; It is expedient for you that I go away: for if I go not away, the Comforter will not come unto you; but if I depart, I will send him unto you. ⁸And when he has come, he will reprove the world of sin, and of righteousness, and of judgment: ⁹Of sin, because they believe not on me; ¹⁰Of righteousness, because I go to my Father, and ye see me no more; ¹¹Of judgment, because the prince of this world is judged. ¹²I have yet many things to say unto you, but ye cannot bear them now. ¹³Howbeit when he, the Spirit of truth, has come, he will guide you into all truth: for he shall not speak of himself; but whatsoever he shall hear, that shall he speak, and he will show you things to come.

God is reminded how humankind needed his Word and his Spirit to move on the water, which is his Word, just as God's Word said this in Genesis 1:2, "And the earth was without form, and void; and darkness was upon the face of the deep. And the Spirit of God moved upon the face of the waters." God knew that his Spirit went together like a living stream and rain, as in Jacob's well.

Jesus said this to his disciples John 4:32, "But he said unto them, 'I have meat to eat that ye know not of.'"

Jesus was on his way to Jacob's well, where he will set up a spiritual meat meal for those to read in the future of the events of the Samaritan woman.

John 4:6–27

> ⁶Now Jacob's well was there. Jesus, therefore, being wearied with his journey, sat thus on the well: and it was about the sixth hour. ⁷There cometh a woman of Samaria to draw water: Jesus saith unto her, Give me to drink. ⁸(For his disciples were gone away unto the city to buy meat.) ⁹Then saith the woman of Samaria unto him, How is it that thou, being a Jew, asks drink of me, which am a woman of Samaria? for the Jews have no dealings with the Samaritans.

¹⁰Jesus answered and said unto her, If thou knewest the gift of God, and who it is that saith to thee, Give me to drink; thou wouldest have asked of him, and he would have given thee living water. ¹¹The woman saith unto him, Sir, thou hast nothing to draw with, and the well is deep: from whence then hast thou that living water? ¹²Art thou greater than our father Jacob, which gave us the well, and drank thereof himself, and his children, and his cattle? ¹³Jesus answered and said unto her, Whosoever drinketh of this water shall thirst again: ¹⁴But whosoever drinketh of the water that I shall give him shall never thirst; but the water that I shall give him shall be in him a well of water springing up into everlasting life. ¹⁵The woman saith unto him, Sir, give me this water, that I thirst not, neither come hither to draw. ¹⁶Jesus saith unto her, Go, call thy husband, and come hither. ¹⁷The woman answered and said, I have no husband. Jesus said unto her, Thou hast well said, I have no husband: ¹⁸For thou hast had five husbands; and he whom thou now hast is not thy husband: in that sadist thou truly. ¹⁹The woman saith unto him, Sir, I perceive that thou art a prophet. ²⁰Our fathers worshipped in this mountain; and ye say, that in Jerusalem is the place where men ought to worship. ²¹Jesus saith unto her, Woman, believe me, the hour cometh, when ye shall neither in this mountain, nor yet at Jerusalem, worship the Father. ²²Ye worship ye know not what: we know what we worship: for salvation is of the Jews. ²³But the hour cometh, and now is, when the true worshippers shall worship the Father in spirit and in truth: for the Father seeketh such to worship him. ²⁴God is a Spirit: and they that worship him must worship him in spirit and in truth. ²⁵The woman saith unto him, I know that Messias cometh, which is called Christ: when he has come, he will tell us all things. ²⁶Jesus saith unto her, I that speak unto thee am he.

The meat that Jesus set up was Jacob's well. Here was Jesus, who is righteous and full of the Holy Ghost, a picture of the Trinity at the well talking to the lady knowing his disciples did not see the spiritual meat, which was Jacob's well; the well itself is made of dirt, and so is humankind.

Ecclesiastes 3:20, "All go unto one place; all are of the dust, and all turn to dust again."

Genesis 2:7, "And the Lord God formed man of the dust of the ground, and breathed into his nostrils the breath of life; and man became a living soul."

The well itself is a picture of humankind, a form of a vessel.

Jacob's well has two sources of water: the stream, which is a picture of living water, and the rainwater, which is a picture of God's Word coming together when they are joined at the merging point. Jesus was standing at a well, which was a picture of himself, full of the Holy Ghost, the Word of God, and in a vessel called flesh.

God is reminded the Word had to become flesh and die for humankind so that humankind could become the Word and die to flesh.

1 Corinthians 15:31, "I protest by your rejoicing which I have in Christ Jesus our Lord, I die daily."

Luke 9:23, "And he said to them all, If any man will come after me, let him deny himself, and take up his cross daily, and follow me."

Romans 6:6, "Knowing this, that our old man is crucified with him, that the body of sin might be destroyed, that henceforth we should not serve sin."

God knows that humankind has to have the Holy Ghost to move on the Word of God because he is the author. The same as God would say, the Holy Ghost moved on the waters.

2 Timothy 3:16, "All scripture is given by inspiration of God, and is profitable for doctrine, for reproof, for correction, for instruction in righteousness."

2 Peter 1:21, "For the prophecy came not in old time by the will of man: but holy men of God spake as they were moved by the Holy Ghost."

When Jesus turns the water into wine, it too was a picture of him.

John 2:5–9

> ⁵His mother saith unto the servants, Whatsoever he saith unto you, do it. ⁶And there were set there six waterpots of stone, after the manner of the purifying of the Jews, containing two or three firkins apiece. ⁷Jesus saith unto them, Fill the waterpots with water. And they filled them up to the brim. ⁸And he saith unto them, Draw out now, and bear unto the governor of the feast. And they bare it. ⁹When the ruler of the feast had tasted the water that was made wine, and knew not whence it was: (but the servants which drew the water knew;) the governor of the feast called the bridegroom,

Now this time it is six vessels, a number I refer to for humankind. The water is a picture of the Word of God, and the win a picture of the Holy Ghost after he has moved on the water in which you and I become Christlike, because of what he did on the cross. And one day his son and daughter will attend a marriage event with him, and he is reminded that the Word of God and the Holy Ghost have become one in us, his children, who praise God.

Romans 8:14, "For as many as are led by the Spirit of God, they are the sons of God."

Galatians 5:18, "But if ye be led of the Spirit, ye are not under the law."

2 Timothy 2:15, "Study to shew thyself approved unto God, a workman that needeth not to be ashamed, rightly dividing the word of truth."

Proverbs 3:5–6, ⁵"Trust in the Lord with all thine heart; and lean not unto thine own understanding. ⁶In all thy ways acknowledge him, and he shall direct thy paths. This is way you have to be born-again."

1 John 5:6, "This is he that came by water and blood, even Jesus Christ; not by water only, but by water and blood. And it is the Spirit that beareth witness, because the Spirit is truth."

God looks at the blue part of the rainbow and is reminded of himself, the Father, and one of the three Godheads, with red being a picture of the Son of God and yellow being the Holy Ghost, the other two parts of the Godhead. These three colors are what make up the other colors as much as that these three parts of God make up all creation; without these three, the rainbow or the Godhead, nothing else can exist.

Father God loves his creation so much, not just because he created humankind, but rather he put a soul in humankind until humankind's souls were murdered by Satan.

Genesis 2:7, "And the Lord God formed man of the dust of the ground, and breathed into his nostrils the breath of life; and man became a living soul."

John 8:44

> Ye are of your father the devil, and the lusts of your father ye will do. He was a murderer from the beginning, and abode not in the truth, because there is no truth in him. When he speaketh a lie, he speaketh of his own: for he is a liar, and the father of it.

There are two events in the scripture that show the three that are one in the Godhead.

Matthew 3:16–17

> [16]And Jesus, when he was baptized, went up straightway out of the water: and, lo, the heavens were opened unto him, and he saw the Spirit of God descending like a dove, and lighting upon him: [17]And lo a voice from heaven, saying, This is my beloved Son, in whom I am well pleased.

This is truly a picture and portrait of the Trinity, the son of God, the Holy Spirit, and God the Father, all in one setting.

Acts 7:55, "But he, being full of the Holy Ghost, looked up stedfastly into heaven, and saw the glory of God, and Jesus standing on the right hand of God."

Here you see the Trinity in a different shape, you got Steven looking at Jesus on the right-hand side of God, and you got Steven looking up, and you got God the son and the Holy Ghost that Steven is full of. This is the picture of the Trinity; the only difference now is we have become sons and daughters of God, so when we pray to the Father in Jesus's name, a child of God is creating the Trinity cycle by talking to the Father in Jesus's name with the Holy Spirit in us, just as when Steven was looking up seeing Jesus on the right-hand side of God and the spirit of God is in him, this is a picture of the Trinity.

God the Father is reminded of what he would have to do as a father to get as many souls as possible back.

John 1:12–13

[12]But as many as received him, to them gave he power to become the sons of God, even to them that believe on his name: [13]Which were born, not of blood, nor of the will of the flesh, nor of the will of man, but of God.

John 15:13–15

> [13]Greater love hath no man than this, that a man lay down his life for his friends. [14]Ye are my friends, if ye do whatsoever I command you. [15]Henceforth I call you not servants; for the servant knowest not what his lord doeth: but I have called you friends; for all things that I have heard of my Father I have made known unto you.

The color orange in the rainbow is a picture of being a brand-new start, new horizon, and even born-again or starting anew.

To get orange you would have to merge red with yellow. It takes both to convert to orange.

When God looked at this color, he was reminded of what was to come later in humankind's history to be able for humankind to be born-again.

His Son Jesus and the Holy Spirit and Word of God, which these two are one, which brings forth new birth to humankind's soul to be able to return to God in fellowship and in heaven. This is the picture of red and yellow, which causes orange to be seen.

1 Peter 1:23–25

> [23]Being born again, not of corruptible seed, but of incorruptible, by the word of God, which liveth and abideth forever. [24]For all flesh is as grass, and all the glory of man as the flower of grass. The grass withereth, and the flower thereof falleth away: [25]But the word of the Lord endureth forever. And this is the word which by the gospel is preached unto you.

John 3:3, "Jesus answered and said unto him, Verily, verily, I say unto thee, Except a man be born again, he cannot see the kingdom of God."

John 3:5, "Jesus answered, Verily, verily, I say unto thee, Except a man be born of water and of the Spirit, he cannot enter into the kingdom of God."

Jesus will give himself to pay for the sins of the world. This is what God sees when he looks at the color red. The water is the Word of God, and the Spirit is the Holy Ghost, which are what God sees when he looks at the color yellow.

When one is born-again and receives the Holy Ghost, then that one would need to read the Word of God to let it become one in one's soul, like rain being the Word of God and a river being the Holy Ghost to become one and flow together. Because God made this possible by sacrificing his son Jesus.

John 3:1–21

> [1]There was a man of the Pharisees, named Nicodemus, a ruler of the Jews: [2]The same came to Jesus by night, and said unto him, Rabbi, we know that thou art a teacher come from God: for no man can do these miracles that thou doest, except God be with him. [3]Jesus answered and said unto him, Verily, verily, I say unto thee, Except a man be born again, he cannot see the kingdom of God. [4]Nicodemus

saith unto him, How can a man be born when he is old? can he enter the second time into his mother's womb, and be born? [5]Jesus answered, Verily, verily, I say unto thee, Except a man be born of water and of the Spirit, he cannot enter into the kingdom of God. [6]That which is born of the flesh is flesh; and that which is born of the Spirit is spirit. [7]Marvel not that I said unto thee, Ye must be born again. [8]The wind bloweth where it listeth, and thou hearest the sound thereof, but canst not tell whence it cometh, and whither it goeth: so is every one that is born of the Spirit. [9]Nicodemus answered and said unto him, How can these things be? [10]Jesus answered and said unto him, Art thou a master of Israel, and knowest not these things? [11]Verily, verily, I say unto thee, We speak that we do know, and testify that we have seen; and ye receive not our witness. [12]If I have told you earthly things, and ye believe not, how shall ye believe, if I tell you of heavenly things? [13]And no man hath ascended up to heaven, but he that came down from heaven, even the Son of man which is in heaven. [14]And as Moses lifted up the serpent in the wilderness, even so must the Son of man be lifted up: [15]That whosoever believeth in him should not perish, but have eternal life. [16]For God so loved the world, that he gave his only begotten Son, that whosoever believeth in him should not perish, but have everlasting life. [17]For God sent not his Son into the world to condemn the world; but that the world through him might be saved. [18]He that believeth on him is not condemned: but he that believeth not is condemned already, because he hath not believed in the name of the only begotten Son of God. [19]And this is the condemnation, that light is come into the world, and men loved darkness rather than light, because their deeds were evil. [20]For everyone that doeth evil hateth the light, neither cometh to the light, lest his deeds should be reproved. [21]But he that doeth truth cometh to the light, that his deeds may be made manifest, that they are wrought in God.

Sin has been paid in full for everyone. All one has to do is believe it to be saved and start the new birth steps. One cannot go any further unless this step is met first.

Acts 16:30–33

> [30]And brought them out, and said, Sirs, what must I do to be saved? [31]And they said, Believe on the Lord Jesus Christ, and thou shalt be saved, and thy house. [32]And they spake unto him the word of the Lord, and to all that were in his house. [33]And he took them the same hour of the night, and washed their stripes; and was baptized, he and all his, straightway.

Romans 10:9–11

> [9]That if thou shalt confess with thy mouth the Lord Jesus, and shalt believe in thine heart that God hath raised him from the dead, thou shalt be saved. [10]For with the heart man believeth unto righteousness; and with the mouth confession is made unto salvation. [11]For the scripture saith, Whosoever believeth on him shall not be ashamed.

This takes faith on this first step to receive salvation. Without faith it is impossible to please God. The moment one believes their faith has started and the Holy Ghost has entered you to merge more of that faith with him, which faith is the Word of God, and from there one starts to grow in faith and the new man gets stronger.

Hebrews 11:6, "But without faith it is impossible to please him: for he that cometh to God must believe that he is, and that he is a rewarder of them that diligently seek him."

Romans 10:17, "So then faith cometh by hearing, and hearing by the word of God."

James 2:14–26

> [14]What doth it profit, my brethren, though a man say he hath faith, and have not works? can faith save him? [15]If a brother or sister be naked, and destitute of daily food, [16]And

one of you say unto them, Depart in peace, be ye warmed and filled; notwithstanding ye give them not those things which are needful to the body; what doth it profit? [17]Even so faith, if it hath not works, is dead, being alone. [18]Yea, a man may say, Thou hast faith, and I have works shew me thy faith without thy works, and I will shew thee my faith by my works. [19]Thou believest that there is one God; thou doest well: the devils also believe, and tremble. [20]But wilt thou know, O vain man, that faith without works is dead? [21]Was not Abraham our father justified by works, when he had offered Isaac his son upon the altar? [22]Seest thou how faith wrought with his works, and by works was faith made perfect? [23]And the scripture was fulfilled which saith, Abraham believed God, and it was imputed unto him for righteousness: and he was called the Friend of God. [24]Ye see then how that by works a man is justified, and not by faith only. [25]Likewise also was not Rahab the harlot justified by works, when she had received the messengers, and had sent them out another way? [26]For as the body without the spirit is dead, so faith without works is dead also.

When one believes that Jesus paid the wages of sin with his lifeblood, then one acts on it, not to be saved, but because one is saved by studying and worshipping and praying and obeying God's Words.

Romans 6:23, "For the wages of sin is death; but the gift of God is eternal life through Jesus Christ our Lord."

2 Timothy 2:15, "Study to shew thyself approved unto God, a workman that needeth not to be ashamed, rightly dividing the word of truth."

Ephesians 2:8–10

[8]For by grace are ye saved through faith; and that not of yourselves: it is the gift of God: [9]Not of works, lest any man should boast. [10]For we are his workmanship, created in Christ Jesus unto good works, which God hath before ordained that we should walk in them.

John 14:15–31

> [15]If ye love me, keep my commandments. [16]And I will pray the Father, and he shall give you another Comforter, that he may abide with you forever; [17]Even the Spirit of truth; whom the world cannot receive, because it seeth him not, neither knowest him: but ye know him; for he dwelleth with you, and shall be in you. [18]I will not leave you comfortless: I will come to you. [19]Yet a little while, and the world seeth me no more; but ye see me: because I live, ye shall live also. [20]At that day ye shall know that I am in my Father, and ye in me, and I in you. [21]He that hath my commandments, and keepeth them, he it is that loveth me: and he that loveth me shall be loved of my Father, and I will love him, and will manifest myself to him. [22]Judas saith unto him, not Iscariot, Lord, how is it that thou wilt manifest thyself unto us, and not unto the world? [23]Jesus answered and said unto him, If a man love me, he will keep my words: and my Father will love him, and we will come unto him, and make our abode with him. [24]He that loveth me not keepeth not my sayings: and the word which ye hear is not mine, but the Father's which sent me. [25]These things have I spoken unto you, being yet present with you. [26]But the Comforter, which is the Holy Ghost, whom the Father will send in my name, he shall teach you all things, and bring all things to your remembrance, whatsoever I have said unto you. [27]Peace I leave with you, my peace I give unto you: not as the world giveth, give I unto you. Let not your heart be troubled, neither let it be afraid. [28]Ye have heard how I said unto you, I go away, and come again unto you. If ye loved me, ye would rejoice, because I said, I go unto the Father: for my Father is greater than I. [29]And now I have told you before it come to pass, that, when it is come to pass, ye might believe.

John 16:33, "These things I have spoken unto you, that in me ye might have peace. In the world ye shall have tribulation: but be of good cheer; I have overcome the world."

God is reminded of the born-again children of God that will be saved during the grace period, even though many will not believe

Matthew 7:14, "Because strait is the gate, and narrow is the way, which leadeth unto life, and few there be that find it."

Now yellow is a picture of the Word of God and the Holy Ghost, and blue is a picture of God our Father that causes the color green to exist and the ability of the new man to grow.

2 Corinthians 5:17, "Therefore if any man be in Christ, he is a new creature: old things are passed away; behold, all things are become new."

Now the growing is what God sees when he looks at green on the rainbow. He is reminded of how all the born-again children of God will have to grow as an infant does.

Jesus is the prime example of a child of God. After all, he was the first begotten Son of God, who knew no sin. He would set the example of every son of God that would follow after him.

2 Corinthians 5:21, "For he hath made him to be sin for us, who knew no sin; that we might be made the righteousness of God in him."

Jesus from the moment that he was planted in his mother Mary, by the Holy Ghost, to his death and resurrection was for us the believers to follow in his footsteps.

Revelation 1:5 And from Jesus Christ, who is the faithful witness, and the first begotten of the dead, and the prince of the kings of the earth. Unto him that loved us, and washed us from our sins in his own blood, Jesus had to complete the journey from his mother belly to his Father in heaven, so those that come after him could do the same.

Jesus is the picture of the new man in his believers, once one believes and their journey is to grow in us as Jesus grew himself.

Just as Mary was seeded by the Holy Ghost and Jesus was delivered and grew until his death on the cross is a picture of the new man in his believer. And his death on the cross allows all that will receive him to become a new man. And as he was resurrected, so will the new man when that time comes.

Matthew 1:18–21

> [18]Now the birth of Jesus Christ was on this wise: When as his mother Mary was espoused to Joseph, before they came together, she was found with child of the Holy Ghost. [19]Then Joseph her husband, being a just man, and not willing to make her a public example, was minded to put her away privily. [20]But while he thought on these things, behold, the angel of the Lord appeared unto him in a dream, saying, Joseph, thou son of David, fear not to take unto thee Mary thy wife: for that which is conceived in her is of the Holy Ghost. [21]And she shall bring forth a son, and thou shalt call his name JESUS: for he shall save his people from their sins.

A baby has to be conceived from seed to birth, and this is the same as the new man.

Luke 1:41–44

> [41]And it came to pass, that, when Elisabeth heard the salutation of Mary, the babe leaped in her womb; and Elisabeth was filled with the Holy Ghost: [42]And she spake out with a loud voice, and said, Blessed art thou among women, and blessed is the fruit of thy womb. [43]And whence is this to me, that the mother of my Lord should come to me? [44]For, lo, as soon as the voice of thy salutation sounded in mine ears, the babe leaped in my womb for joy.

A baby has to drink milk and grow before they can eat meat, and this is the same with the new man.

Luke 2:7, "And she brought forth her firstborn son, and wrapped him in swaddling clothes, and laid him in a manger, because there was no room for them in the inn."

1 Peter 2:1–3

> [1]Wherefore laying aside all malice, and all guile, and hypocrisies, and envies, and all evil speakings, [2]As newborn babes, desire the sincere milk of the word, that ye may grow thereby: [3]If so be ye have tasted that the Lord is gracious.

Hebrews 5:13–14 [13]For everyone that useth milk is unskilful in the word of righteousness: for he is a babe. [14]But strong meat belongeth to them that are of full age, even those who by reason of use have their senses exercised to discern both good and evil.

1 Corinthians 3:1–3

> [1]And I, brethren, could not speak unto you as unto spiritual, but as unto carnal, even as unto babes in Christ. [2]I have fed you with milk, and not with meat: for hitherto ye were not able to bear it, neither yet now are ye able. [3]For ye are yet carnal: for whereas there is among you envying, and strife, and divisions, are ye not carnal, and walk as men?

Now as the new man grows, he is able to eat meat spiritually

Luke 2:52, "And Jesus increased in wisdom and stature, and in favour with God and man."

1 Corinthians 10:2–3, [2]"And were all baptized unto Moses in the cloud and in the sea; [3]And did all eat the same spiritual meat."

Then one is able to go forth and do as God has called him or her to do in this life.

Matthew 4:17, "From that time Jesus began to preach, and to say, Repent: for the kingdom of heaven is at hand."

2 Timothy 4:6–8

> [6]For I am now ready to be offered, and the time of my departure is at hand. [7]I have fought a good fight, I have finished my course, I have kept the faith: [8]Henceforth there is laid up for me a crown of righteousness, which the Lord,

the righteous judge, shall give me at that day: and not to me only, but unto all them also that love his appearing.

Jesus is the example of how a new man should grow spiritually

Mark 15:37, "And Jesus cried with a loud voice, and gave up the ghost."

God is reminded of his children's birth, growth, and departure and also knows we as believers might fall or stumble, and just like any father, he would make a way.

1 John 2:1–2

> ¹My little children, these things write I unto you, that ye sin not. And if any man sin, we have an advocate with the Father, Jesus Christ the righteous: ²And he is the propitiation for our sins: and not for ours only, but also for the sins of the whole world.

1 John 1:9, "If we confess our sins, he is faithful and just to forgive us our sins, and to cleanse us from all unrighteousness."

Red is a picture of the blood of Jesus and blue a picture of God the Father. These colors create purple, which is a picture of righteousness and royalty.

God is reminded of how he has a family of royalty that will be gathered around him forever.

Ephesians 1:5, "Having predestinated us unto the adoption of children by Jesus Christ to himself, according to the good pleasure of his will, God is reminded of all he has for those that love him."

1 Corinthians 2:9, "But as it is written, Eye hath not seen, nor ear heard, neither have entered into the heart of man, the things which God hath prepared for them that love him."

1 Peter 2:9, "But ye are a chosen generation, a royal priesthood, an holy nation, a peculiar people; that ye should shew forth the praises of him who hath called you out of darkness into his marvelous light."

The new names he will give to them which are his.

Revelation 2:17

> He that hath an ear, let him hear what the Spirit saith unto the churches; To him that overcometh will I give to eat of the hidden manna, and will give him a white stone, and in the stone a new name written, which no man knoweth saving he that receiveth it.

The eternal body that will be given out to believers.

Philippians 3:21, "Who shall change our vile body, that it may be fashioned like unto his glorious body, according to the working whereby he is able even to subdue all things unto himself."

The titles he will give and positions to those that believe.

1 Corinthians 6:2–3

> [2]Do ye not know that the saints shall judge the world? and if the world shall be judged by you, are ye unworthy to judge the smallest matters? [3]Know ye not that we shall judge angels? how much more things that pertain to this life?

Revelation 1:5–6

> [5]And from Jesus Christ, who is the faithful witness, and the first begotten of the dead, and the prince of the kings of the earth. Unto him that loved us, and washed us from our sins in his own blood, [6]And hath made us kings and priests unto God and his Father; to him be glory and dominion for ever and ever. Amen.

God looks on this bow and is reminded of the past, present, and future, the beginning and the end, the first and the last.

1 Corinthians 15:45–47

> [45]And so it is written, The first man Adam was made a living soul; the last Adam was made a quickening spirit. [46]Howbeit that was not first which is spiritual, but that which is natural;

and afterward that which is spiritual. [47]The first man is of the earth, earthy; the second man is the Lord from heaven.

Revelation 1:8, "I am Alpha and Omega, the beginning and the ending, saith the Lord, which is, and which was, and which is to come, the Almighty."

Revelation 22:12, "And, behold, I come quickly; and my reward is with me, to give every man according as his work shall be."

The bow has a lot to say; one just needs to listen, and one can hear the bow speak clearly.

Matthew 11:15, "He that hath ears to hear, let him hear."

www.ingramcontent.com/pod-product-compliance
Lightning Source LLC
Chambersburg PA
CBHW041625140626

46547CB00030B/1000